Jacob's Ladder
Reading Comprehension Program

GRADE 3

Nonfiction

Jacob's Ladder
Reading Comprehension Program

GRADE 3

Nonfiction

Tamra Stambaugh, Ph.D., &
Joyce VanTassel-Baska, Ed.D.

Routledge
Taylor & Francis Group

NEW YORK AND LONDON

First published in 2016 by Prufrock Press Inc.

Published in 2021 by Routledge
605 Third Avenue, New York, NY 10017
2 Park Square, Milton Park, Abingdon, Oxon OX14 4RN

Routledge is an imprint of the Taylor & Francis Group, an informa business

Copyright © 2016 by Taylor & Francis Group

Cover and layout design by Raquel Trevino

All rights reserved. No part of this book may be reprinted or reproduced or utilised in any form or by any electronic, mechanical, or other means, now known or hereafter invented, including photocopying and recording, or in any information storage or retrieval system, without permission in writing from the publishers.

Notice:
Product or corporate names may be trademarks or registered trademarks, and are used only for identification and explanation without intent to infringe.

ISBN: 9781618215543 (pbk)

DOI: 10.4324/9781003236047

Table of Contents

Acknowledgments vii

Part I: Teachers' Guide to Jacob's Ladder
Reading Comprehension Program 1

Part II: Readings and Student Ladder Sets by Discipline . . 23
    Section 1: Science 25
    Section 2: Math 49
    Section 3: Social Studies 65

Part III: Readings and Student Ladder Sets
for Fiction and Nonfiction Comparisons 99

Appendix A: Pre- and Postassessments
With Scoring Rubric 131

Appendix B: Record-Keeping Forms/Documents 141

Appendix C: Alignment of the New Nonfiction Jacob's
Ladder Program to the CCSS-ELA Standards 151

About the Authors 157

Acknowledgments

We would like to thank Lacy Compton and Stephanie McCauley from Prufrock Press for their unwavering support of this project and their dedication to helping us find appropriate nonfiction selections for this series. If age-appropriate passages were not available, they often rewrote items or found alternatives on similar topics. Their patience, responsiveness, and hard work are most appreciated.

Part I: Teachers' Guide to Jacob's Ladder Reading Comprehension Program

Rationale

Decoding and constructing meaning of the written word are two of the earliest tasks required of students in schools. These skills occupy the central place in the curriculum at the elementary level. Yet approaches to teaching reading comprehension often are "skill and drill," using worksheets on low-level reading material. As a result, students frequently are unable to transfer these skills from exercise pages and apply them to new, higher level reading material.

The time expended to ensure that students become autonomous and advanced readers would suggest the need for a methodology that deliberately moves students from simple to complex reading skills with texts matched to reading level as determined by Lexile and other approaches to ensure appropriate reading challenges. Such a learning approach to reading skill development ensures that students can traverse easily from basic comprehension skills to higher level critical reading skills, while using the same reading stimulus to navigate this transition. Reading comprehension and knowledge acquisition are enhanced by instructional scaffolding, using strategies and processes to help students analyze passages (Villaume & Brabham, 2002). In addition, teachers who emphasize higher order thinking through questions and tasks (like those applied in this program) promote greater reading growth (Taylor, Pearson, Peterson, & Rodriguez, 2003), especially when this instruction is presented through inquiry and discussion as opposed to isolated worksheet-like activities. Cognitive science suggests that students need to have purpose and direction for discussions of text to yield meaningful learning and that scaffolding is a necessary part of enhancing critical reading behavior and developing expertise (Bransford, Brown, & Cocking, 2000).

The Jacob's Ladder Reading Comprehension Program: Nonfiction series was written in response to teacher findings that students have a deep curiosity to learn more about the world around them, but need more developmentally appropriate materials and scaffolding to process and accurately interpret informational texts (Duke, Bennett-Armistead, & Roberts, 2003; VanTassel-Baska & Stambaugh, 2006a). Tivnan and Hemphill (2005) studied reading reform curricula in Title I schools and found that few of the reading programs emphasized skills beyond basic phonemic awareness, fluency, or limited comprehension. To compound this, many popularized reading curricula include less than 20% informational reading selections (Duke et al., 2003). For students who are in the lowest SES schools, even less access to informational texts is available (Duke et al., 2003; Moss, 2005). Therefore, supplementary curriculum at the elementary level that is focused on higher level thinking skills with access to engaging informational texts is greatly needed.

With the onset of Common Core State Standards (CCSS) and other curriculum reform initiatives, there has been an increased emphasis on nonfiction reading. Advocates suggest that by fourth grade students should be reading 50% literacy texts and 50% informational texts as part of their repertoire. The number of nonfiction texts to be read increases to 70% of all readings for graduating, college-ready seniors (Calkins, Ehrenworth, & Lehman, 2012). The incorporation of engaging nonfiction texts into an already rigorous reading curriculum is found to motivate students—especially reluctant readers and those with innate curiosity and precocity in a specific content domain. Moreover, the use of nonfiction increases knowledge and access to information beyond the classroom walls and encourages engagement in the practice of becoming lifelong learners (Moss, 2005).

Jacob's Ladder Reading Comprehension Program: Nonfiction (Jacob's Ladder: Nonfiction) is a compilation of the instructional scaffolding and reading exercises necessary to aid students in their journey toward becoming critical and inquisitive readers. Students learn concept development skills through generalizing, predicting and forecasting skills through delineating implications of events/perspectives/situations, comparative analysis skills through discerning textual meaning and author's purpose, and creative analysis skills through synthesizing information and producing new products or ideas (VanTassel-Baska & Stambaugh, 2006a). The questions and tasks for each reading are open-ended, allowing for multiple responses that ultimately improve performance on comprehension tests (Guthrie, Schafer, & Huang, 2001). Progressing through the hierarchy of skills also requires students to reread the text, thereby improving meta-comprehension accuracy (Rawson, Dunlosky, & Thiede, 2000). As many gifted students are able to assimilate information more quickly and make connections within and across disciplines, a comparative analysis of a variety of nonfiction texts supports their development and content acquisition (Rogers, 2007). In addition, the more diverse works students have accessible to read, the more likely they are to show higher achievement gains in addition to reading engagement (Brozo, Shiel, & Topping, 2007).

Introduction to Jacob's Ladder: Nonfiction

Jacob's Ladder: Nonfiction is a supplemental reading program that implements targeted readings adapted primarily from blogs, newspapers, speeches, scientific journals, and biography study. With this program, students engage in an inquiry process that moves from lower order to higher order thinking skills. Starting with basic textual understanding, students learn to critically analyze texts by determining implications and consequences, generalizations, main ideas, vocabulary of the discipline, emotional appeals, and/or creative synthesis. This book is suggested for gifted or high-achieving students in grade 3. It is used to enhance reading comprehension and critical thinking. Tasks are organized into six skill ladders, A–F, and each ladder focuses on a different set of skills. Students "climb" each ladder by answering lower level questions and then moving to higher level questions (or rungs) at the top of each ladder. As many gifted students are more conceptual and prefer whole to part learning (Rogers, 2007), it is also appropriate to begin at the highest rung and scaffold down as needed to ensure that students have mastered the necessary skills. However, each ladder may stand alone as it focuses on a separate critical thinking component in reading. The intent of the ladder design is that students spend more time discussing ideas at the top of the ladder rungs instead of the bottom rungs, although each rung is distinct in its purpose for skill development.

Ladder A focuses on implications and consequences at the highest and most abstract level. By leading students through sequencing and cause-and-effect activities, students learn to draw implications and consequences from readings. Ladder B focuses on making generalizations. Students first learn to provide details and examples and then move to classifying and organizing those details in order to move up to the highest level of making generalizations. Ladder C focuses on themes. Students begin by identifying key literary features or questions about a text and then make inferences about a given textually based situation. Ladder D focuses at the highest level on creative synthesis by leading students through paraphrasing and summarizing activities. Ladder E focuses on students' emotional responses or reactions to the text as well as analyzing emotional appeals that may be evident in some informational readings by distinguishing emotion and fact, and then channeling the information productively. Ladder F provides an emphasis on word choice and vocabulary of the discipline by engaging learners in understanding, applying, and embedding new vocabulary or analyzing appropriate word choice in both their own and others' writing. Ladders are carefully matched to each text, based on the key thinking skills that are implicit or explicit within the readings.

Table 1 provides a visual representation of the six ladders and corresponding objectives for each ladder and rung.

Ladder A: Focus on Implications and Consequences

The goal of Ladder A is to develop prediction and forecasting skills by encouraging students to make connections among the information provided. Starting with sequencing, students learn to recognize basic types of change or sequence of details that occur within a text. Through identifying cause and effect relationships, students then can judge the impact of certain events, perspectives, contexts, or problems. Finally, through recognizing consequences and implications, students predict or analyze positive, negative, or short- and long-term consequences by judging probable outcomes based on data provided. The rungs are as follows:

- **Ladder A, Rung 1, Sequencing:** The lowest rung on the ladder, sequencing, requires students to organize a set of information in order, based on their reading (e.g., List the steps of a recipe in order.).

- **Ladder A, Rung 2, Cause and Effect:** The middle rung, cause and effect, requires students to think about relationships and identify what causes certain effects and/or what effects were brought about because of certain causes (e.g., What causes a cake to rise in the oven? What effect does the addition of egg yolks have on a batter?).

- **Ladder A, Rung 3, Consequences and Implications:** The highest rung on Ladder A requires students to think about both short- and long-term or positive and negative events that may happen as a result of an effect they have identified (e.g., What are the short-

TABLE 1
Goals and Objectives of Jacob's Ladder Nonfiction Thinking Skills by Ladder and Rung

A3: Consequences and Implications	B3: Generalizations	C3: Theme/Concept	D3: Creative Synthesis	E3: Using Emotion	F3: Playing With Words
Students will be able to explain and predict the short-/long-term or positive/negative implications of an event, problem, solution, perspective, or passage.	Students will be able to write and/or justify generalized (conceptual) statements about a reading and/or an idea within or across readings, using data to support their suppositions.	Students will be able to identify a major idea or theme common throughout the text or series of texts.	Students will create something new using what they have learned from the reading (or series of readings) and their synopses.	Students will be able to analyze how emotion affects the passage and/or the reader.	Students will be able to accurately apply strategies to make an argument, express a point, or use domain-specific vocabulary in a different context or their own creation.

A2: Cause and Effect	B2: Classifications	C2: Inference	D2: Summarizing	E2: Expressing Emotion	F2: Thinking About Words
Students will be able to identify relationships between events, contexts, problems, solutions, or other phenomena.	Students will be able to categorize different aspects of the text or identify and sort categories from a list of topics or details.	Students will be able to use textual clues to make judgments about specific textual events, ideas, or the author's purpose.	Students will be able to provide a synopsis of text sections.	Students will be able to articulate their feelings about a passage or concept expressed within a passage through a variety of media (e.g., song, art, poem, story, essay, speech).	Students will be able to analyze the use of words or devices used to craft a message as related to the theme or idea of a text.

A1: Sequencing	B1: Details	C1: Textual Elements and Understanding	D1: Paraphrasing	E1: Understanding Emotion	F1: Understanding Words
Students will be able to list, in order of importance or occurrence in the text, specific events or perspectives.	Students will be able to list specific details or recall facts related to the text or generate a list of ideas about a specific topic or event given evidence.	Students will be able to identify and explain specific elements, such as context, organization, and general understanding of discipline-specific ideas within a given source.	Students will be able to restate lines read using their own words.	Students will be able to explain how emotion and feeling are conveyed in a text and how that may or may not be linked to their personal experience.	Students will be able to identify and define new vocabulary or ideas within the context of a selected passage through the use of context clues.

| Ladder A | Ladder B | Ladder C | Ladder D | Ladder E | Ladder F |

and long-term consequences of baking at home?). Students learn to draw consequences and implications from the text for application in the real world.

Ladder B: Focus on Generalizations

The goal of Ladder B is to help students develop deductive reasoning skills, moving from concrete elements to abstract ideas. Students begin by learning the importance of concrete details and how they can be organized. By the top rung, students are able to make general statements spanning a topic, discipline, or concept. The rungs are as follows:

- **Ladder B, Rung 1, Details:** The lowest rung on Ladder B, details, requires students to list examples or details from what they have read and/or to list examples they know from the real world or have read about (e.g., Make a list of types of transportation. Write as many as you can think of in 2 minutes.).

- **Ladder B, Rung 2, Classifications:** The middle rung of Ladder B, classifications, focuses on students' ability to categorize examples and details based on characteristics (e.g., How might we categorize the modes of transportation you identified?). This activity builds students' skills in categorization and classification.

- **Ladder B, Rung 3, Generalizations:** The highest rung on Ladder B, generalizations, requires students to use the list and categories generated at Rungs 1 and 2 to develop two to three general statements that apply to *all* of their examples (e.g., Write three true statements about transportation.).

Ladder C: Focus on Themes

The goal of Ladder C is to develop literary analysis skills based on an understanding of literary elements. After completing Ladder C, students state the main themes and ideas of the text after identifying setting, characters, and the context of the piece. The rungs for this ladder are as follows:

- **Ladder C, Rung 1, Textual Elements:** While working on the lowest rung of Ladder C, textual elements, students identify and/or describe the elements, such as the author's purpose or organization of the text. This rung also requires students to develop an understanding of a given perspective, idea, or context (e.g., How does the time period when this piece was written help us understand the purpose?).

- **Ladder C, Rung 2, Inference:** The middle rung of Ladder C, inference, requires students to think through a situation in the text and come to a conclusion based on the information and clues provided (e.g., What evidence exists to suggest that this speech is about the interaction of peace and war?).

- **Ladder C, Rung 3, Theme/Concept:** The highest rung of Ladder C, theme/concept, requires students to determine the central idea or theme of a reading. This exercise necessitates that the students explain an idea from the reading that best states what the text means (e.g., What is the author's perspective on the following statement: "There can be no peace without war"? How are these themes portrayed through the speech? What additional concepts are discussed?).

Ladder D: Focus on Creative Synthesis

The goal of Ladder D is to help students develop skills in creative synthesis in order to foster students' creation of new material based on information from the reading. It moves from the level of restating ideas to creating new ideas or synthesizing multiple ideas into something new about a topic or concept. The rungs are as follows:

- **Ladder D, Rung 1, Paraphrasing:** The lowest rung on Ladder D is paraphrasing. This rung requires students to restate a short passage using their own words (e.g., Explain, in your own words, how a supernova is formed.).

- **Ladder D, Rung 2, Summarizing:** Summarizing, the middle rung on Ladder D, requires students to summarize larger sections of text by selecting the most important key points within the text (e.g., In three sentences or less, summarize the purpose of this news release about supernovas.).

- **Ladder D, Rung 3, Creative Synthesis:** The highest rung on Ladder D requires students to create something new using what they have learned from the reading and their synopses of it (e.g., Create a visual that would complement this news piece and help others better understand the main idea the author is trying to convey.).

Ladder E: Focus on Emotional Development

The goal of Ladder E is to help students develop skills in using their emotional intelligence in order to regulate and modulate behavior with respect to learning and to observe how others use emotional appeal in their writings to evoke emotion. It moves from students' understanding of emotion in self and others, to expressing emotion, to channeling emotion for cognitive ends. There is potential for teachers to use this ladder with many primary source documents—in particular, editorial cartoons and speeches. The rungs are as follows:

- **Ladder E, Rung 1, Understanding Emotion:** The lowest rung on Ladder E focuses on understanding emotion in oneself and others. This requires students to identify emotions in the text and relate them to their own lives (e.g., How did the author of this speech use key scenarios or ideas to evoke emotion?). It also requires them to recognize emotional situations and pinpoint the nature of the emotions involved and what is causing them.

- **Ladder E, Rung 2, Expressing Emotion:** The middle rung on Ladder E, expressing emotion, asks students to express emotion in response to their reading of various selections (e.g., How did this speech appeal to you? How did the author try to appeal to his or her audience? Rewrite the speech in a way that would better appeal to you or others of this time period and include a justification for why you included certain emotional appeals.). Teachers may want to substitute kinesthetic responses in the form of dance or skits that demonstrate an emotional reaction to the selections. Art or music of the day can be great extensions to historical and biographical studies that incorporate this ladder.

- **Ladder E, Rung 3, Using Emotion:** The highest rung on Ladder E, using emotion, encourages students to begin regulating emotion for specific purposes (e.g., Write a letter to the editor expressing your reaction to this excerpt that includes appropriate facts and other compelling evidence and emotional appeals.). In application to nonfiction, students need to demonstrate a clear understanding of how to use emotion effectively for accomplishing specific ends, whether through giving a speech or writing a passionate letter in defense of an idea. The deliberate incorporation of emotion in one's communication is stressed.

Ladder F: Focus on Word Study and Vocabulary of the Discipline

In the Jacob's Ladder: Nonfiction series, Ladder F focuses on word study and vocabulary of the discipline. The goal of Ladder F is to move students from understanding meanings of words to appropriately using words within an applicable context or their own creation.

- **Ladder F, Rung 1, Understanding Words:** The lowest rung on Ladder F focuses on understanding words. It requires students to consider how words are used in the context of the story to promote meaning (e.g., How might you determine what the word *condensation* means through context clues and visual representations provided?). Through textual evidence and informational text features, students find new examples or uses of content-specific words and learn how to recognize and use these words appropriately in other contexts.

- **Ladder F, Rung 2, Thinking About Words:** The middle rung of Ladder F, thinking about words, requires students to think about how the key words or text features studied in the first rung enhance the meaning of the text. Students engage in analyzing author word choice in historical documents or deciphering how to apply new content-specific vocabulary into new situations in scientific articles (e.g., Why did the author choose to use the word *crisis* instead of *tragedy*?).

- **Ladder F, Rung 3, Playing With Words:** The highest rung on Ladder F, playing with words, engages students in reflecting on key words or literary elements and applying them to new situations or contexts. Students are asked to apply the new learning to other writing pieces (e.g., Write your own news blog that teaches second graders about the interaction between condensation and evaporation using what you learned from this text as well as two others that you choose; use new ideas and visuals.), and to select the most important aspects of language or other representations for their own use to meaningfully convey ideas.

Process Skills

Along with the six goals addressed by the ladders, a seventh goal focusing on process skills is incorporated in the Jacob's Ladder curriculum. The aim of this goal is to promote learning through interaction and discussion of reading material in the classroom. After completing the ladders and following guidelines for discussion and teacher feedback, students will be able to:

- articulate their understanding of a text using textual support;
- engage in proper dialogue about the meaning or purpose of a selection, including adding their opinion or perspective, with evidence; and
- discuss varied ideas about the intention of a passage both orally and in writing.

Intended Audience: Who Should Use Jacob's Ladder

Although the program is targeted for gifted learners and advanced students who need more exposure to higher level thinking skills in reading, the program may be suitable for other learners as well, including those who are twice-exceptional, students from poverty, and those from different cultural backgrounds (VanTassel-Baska & Stambaugh, 2006b). The Jacob's Ladder: Nonfiction series consists of three levels: Grade 3, Grade 4, and Grade 5. (See also the Jacob's Ladder Reading Comprehension Program series, which focuses primarily on fiction sources available for students in grades K–8.) However, teachers may find that they want to vary usage beyond the recommended levels, depending on students' abilities. Evidence suggests that the curriculum can be successfully implemented with gifted and advanced learners as well as other students (Stambaugh, 2007), depending on the level of scaffolding and grade-level choices (e.g., teachers may go up or down a few grade levels based on their students' needs and readiness levels). Thus, the levels vary and overlap to provide opportunities for teachers to select the most appropriate set of readings for meaningful differentiation for their learners' needs.

Organization of Reading Selections

Each nonfiction book contains two main reading sections: nonfiction by discipline and fiction/nonfiction comparative analyses. The nonfiction section includes readings from a variety of disciplines such as mathematics, science, the arts, and social studies. The comparative fiction section pairs poetry readings with companion nonfiction texts such as biography study or a similar/contrasting article that complements the fiction selection in respect to topic or theme. Sometimes, there is another nonfiction piece used for comparison if it represents another type of writing. For example, in science, students may read two different nonfiction pieces about a similar phenomenon and answer questions about each piece individually, and then respond to a ladder or question set that compares and contrasts the two pieces. A listing of readings by discipline and ladder appears in Table 2. Care was taken to incorporate readings from multiple perspectives, stakeholders, disciplines, events, time periods, and cultures as available.

Research Base

A quasi-experimental study was conducted using Jacob's Ladder as a supplementary program for grade 3–5 students in Title I schools. After receiving professional development, teachers were instructed to implement the Jacob's Ladder curriculum in addition to their basal reading series and guided reading groups. Nonfiction selections were included as part of this study in addition to poetry and fiction selections.

Findings ($N = 495$) suggested that when compared to students who used the basal reader only, those students who were exposed to the Jacob's Ladder curriculum showed significant gains in reading comprehension and critical thinking. Likewise, students who used the curriculum showed significant and important growth on curriculum-based assessments that included determining implications and consequences, making inferences, outlining themes and generalizations, and applying creative synthesis. Students reported greater interest in reading and alluded that the curriculum made them "think harder." Teachers reported more in-depth student discussion and personal growth in the ability to ask open-ended questions in reading (Stambaugh, 2007). The same ladders, models, and goals have been applied to this book. An earlier study also documented the growth in reading comprehension and critical thinking that resulted from using the program with gifted students (French, 2006). It is important to note that success of the program and the impact on student achievement occurred under the conditions of ongoing monitoring of program fidelity that included professional development, modeling, and teacher feedback. Thus teachers should try to implement the program as faithfully as possible with respect to its audience and purposes.

TABLE 2
List of Readings and Ladders by Discipline

Part II: Readings and Student Ladder Sets by Discipline			
Section	**Reading Titles**	**Ladders**	**Comparison Ladder**
Science	The Search for the Ninth Planet	D	
	The Aerodynamics of Crickets	A	B
	Bumblebee Watch	A	B
	A Pox on You!	B, D	
	In Tests of Mathematical Ability, Wolves Lead the Pack Over Dogs	D	
	Grace Murray Hopper, Computer Scientist	A, B	
Math	Making Math Fun	A, D	
	An Introduction to Magic Squares	D	
	Counting Like a Greek	C, D	
	Should Students Use Calculators During Math?	A, D	
Social Studies	Surrender Speech	C	D
	The Fight for the Nez Perce Indian Territory	A	D
	The Struggles of Young Factory Workers in the Industrial Revolution	A	
	Propaganda Posters and World War II	B, C	B
	With God's Help, We Shall Prevail	C	B
	Above and Beyond: Doris "Dorie" Miller and Pearl Harbor	C	
	A New Kind of Snow Day for Students	A, C	
	Should Students Be Required to Wear School Uniforms?	A, D	
Part III: Readings and Student Ladder Sets for Fiction and Nonfiction Comparisons			
Section	**Reading Titles**	**Ladders**	**Comparison Ladder**
Fiction and Nonfiction Comparison	The Decision to Go to the Moon But Outer Space	C C, F	C
	Afternoon on a Hill Solvay Process Company Photograph	C B, D	B
	Good Books Bringing Literature to the Streets	C, F A	D
	The Vain Jackdaw Sandra Cisneros	C C, E	C

Implementation Considerations

Teachers need to consider certain issues when implementing the Jacob's Ladder curriculum. Because modeling, coaching, and feedback appear to enhance student growth in reading and writing (Pressley et al., 2001; Taylor, Peterson, Pearson, & Rodriguez, 2002), it is recommended that teachers review how to complete the task ladders with the entire class at least once, outlining expectations as well as modeling the process prior to assigning small-group or independent work. As students gain more confidence in the curriculum, teachers should allow more independent work coupled with small-group or paired discussion, and then whole-group sharing with teacher feedback. Jacob's Ladder is *not* intended to be used as a set of worksheets or individual tasks, but rather for the facilitation of ongoing discussion and reasoning among groups of learners from dyads to whole-class discussion groups. The material was designed, however, for advanced readers who can independently read the material and comprehend it. It may be the case that, after trying it with the whole class, there needs to be a fallback position to using it only with a small group who needs accelerated resources and scaffolding.

Completing these activities in dyads or small groups will facilitate discussions that stress collaborative reasoning, thereby fostering greater engagement and higher level thinking (Chin, Anderson, & Waggoner, 2001; Harvey, 2002; Pressley et al., 2001; Taylor et al., 2002). The readings and accompanying ladder questions and activities may be organized into a reading center in the classroom or utilized with reading groups during guided reading for those students who need extensions or substitutions to the regular curriculum. Teachers may also choose to read the selections aloud to students in advanced-level reading groups or to the entire class and solicit responses through methods like think-pair-share, whole-group class discussion, or small-group/individual assignments to be completed prior to engaging in a reading group.

Process of Jacob's Ladder

The process of inquiry and feedback, as led and modeled by the teacher, is critical to the success of the program and student mastery of process skills. Teachers need to solicit multiple student responses and encourage dialogue about various perspectives and interpretations of a given text, requiring students to justify their answers with textual support and concrete examples (VanTassel-Baska & Stambaugh, 2006a, 2006b). Sample follow-up questions for helping students engage in discussion, such as those listed below, can be used by the teacher and posted in the classroom to guide students' dialogue. These questions in no way substitute for advanced, content-specific questions, nor do they insinuate that there are no "correct" answers. The purpose of teaching these stems encourages students to engage in dialogue and Socratic seminars while being good consumers of text instead of passive listeners who do not move beyond the basic information within a text.

- That's interesting; does anyone have a **different idea**?
- What in the text provides **evidence** for your thinking?
- What do you think the author **means** by . . . ?
- What do you think are the **implications or consequences** of . . . ?
- Does anyone have a different **point of view**? Justify your answer.
- Tell me more about **why** . . .
- Do you notice any **key words** that might be significant? Why?
- How does this text help us **better understand** . . . ?
- I **agree/disagree** with . . . **because** . . .

Beck and McKeown (1998) suggested that academic discourse in reading promotes textual understanding. They recommended guiding students through the text by showing them how to *mark key words* in a text both on their own and as part of whole-group modeling. Teachers are also encouraged to *reframe student responses* in order to ensure that students have a clear voice that is heard and acknowledged as important to understanding. Knowing that teacher stance is critical to the process of reasoning and understanding, teachers are encouraged to help students use evidence from the text to justify responses, including *turning back in the text* to show where ideas were found. Teachers should also *model* metacognitive approaches by thinking aloud about how one may go about developing an idea or comment, *providing annotations* or background information as necessary, and then *synthesizing key ideas* expressed during a discussion. This guidance will promote critical thinking when combined with the discourse of also asking targeted, open-ended questions to help students gain understanding for themselves without being told what to think.

In order for students to maximize their understanding and engagement in reading nonfiction texts, they must see nonfiction as a way to answer their own questions or appeal to their curious nature (Harvey, 2002; Moss & Hendershot, 2002). Some of the challenges when implementing nonfiction reading selections into the curriculum include finding information that is just right for student engagement (i.e., not too hard or not written in a way that does not allow for engagement and understanding), allowing students to have some choice in the types of informational texts or topics they read, and finding time to allow students to investigate and learn new information (Calkins et al., 2012). Allowing students choice in their reading selections and encouraging students to find ways to answer their own questions has been shown to promote engagement, motivation, and more reading of nonfiction texts for all students (Moss & Hendershot, 2002). The Jacob's Ladder nonfiction texts have been selected to complement the general curriculum and to engage students in reading selections that encourage their higher level thinking and broaden their knowledge of information in a variety of disciplines.

For gifted students and other high-ability learners, the process of curriculum compacting allows for students to test out of basic skills and then work on topics of interest. Teachers may compact certain areas of the curriculum and engage students in posing their own questions. Teachers may match student questions to passages within the Jacob's Ladder text or other nonfiction texts, using the ladder framework. The texts do not need to be used in order but may be mixed or matched to student interests and needs. Of course, the curriculum may also be used to teach students how to read and analyze informational texts as they engage in their own line of inquiry.

Grouping and Jacob's Ladder

Jacob's Ladder may be used in a number of different grouping patterns. The program should be introduced initially as a whole-group activity directed by the teacher with appropriate open-ended questions, feedback, and monitoring. After students have examined each type of ladder with teacher guidance, they should be encouraged to use the program by listing key ideas/thoughts independently (not writing out full sentences or paragraphs for each rung), sharing with a partner, and then discussing their findings with a group as part of eliciting different perspectives. The dyad approach provides maximum opportunities for student discussion of the readings and collaborative decisions about the answers to questions posed. One purpose of the program is to solicit meaningful discussion of the text, which is best accomplished in small groups of students at similar reading levels (VanTassel-Baska & Little, 2017). Meta-analyses of the research on grouping practices continue to support instructional grouping in reading as an important part of successful implementation of a reading program for gifted and high-ability learners (Rogers, 2002, 2007).

Demonstrating Growth: Pre- and Postassessments and Student Products

The preassessment and postassessment included in Appendix A were designed as a diagnostic-prescriptive approach to guide program implementation of Jacob's Ladder. The pretest should be administered, scored, and then used to guide student instruction and the selection of readings for varied ability groups. Both assessments and the scoring rubric are included in Appendix A.

In both the pre- and postassessments, students read a short passage and respond to three questions. Question 1 focuses on understanding implications and consequences of the text. Question 2 assesses students' knowledge of key ideas. Question 3 examines students' ability to make connections and inferences provided in the text, and Question 4 measures students' ability to synthesize information acquired. Jacob's Ladder: Nonfiction, Grade 3 incorporates a preassessment and a postassessment, using biographies as the selected reading.

Upon conclusion of the program or as a midpoint check, the postassessment may be administered to compare to the preassessment results and to measure growth in students' responses. These pre-post results may be used as part of a student portfolio, in a parent-teacher conference, or as documentation of curriculum effectiveness and student progress.

Record-keeping sheets for differentiation within the class are provided in Appendix B. On these forms, teachers record student progress on a 3-point scale: 3 (*applies skills very effectively*), 2 (*understands and applies skills*), or a 1 (*needs more practice with the given skill set*) across readings and ladder sets. These forms may be used as part of a diagnostic-prescriptive approach for selecting more reading materials and ladders based on student understanding or the need for more practice. After teachers administer the preassessment, they may select readings commensurate with key ladder skills needed by individual students and then flexibly group those students according to their levels of understanding of a particular thinking skill. Other forms in Appendix B include blank ladder rungs for students to jot down their answers in preparation for group discussion and metacognitive reflection sheets. The blank ladder rungs for recording answers are not to be used as worksheets that require full sentence responses, but instead as an organizer of thinking or quick outline/bullet points of what students choose to discuss in small- or whole-group debriefing. The metacognitive reflection sheets may be used periodically throughout the program as a way for students to monitor their own growth in thinking and to reflect upon the Jacob's Ladder thinking processes.

Grading and Monitoring Student Understanding

Teachers will want to check student answers as ladder segments are completed and conduct an individual or small-group consultation, similar to a writers' workshop format, to ensure that students understand why their answers may be effective or ineffective. In order to analyze student responses and progress across the program, teachers need to monitor student performance, providing specific comments about student work to promote growth and understanding of content. However, the program was *not* intended for students to write down their ideas to every question. Part of the richness of the program comes in student discussions and interactions with the teacher who models key ideas and strategies.

Grading the ladders and responses is at the teacher's discretion. Teachers should not overemphasize the lower rungs in graded activities. Lower rungs are intended partially as a vehicle to the higher level questions at the top of the ladder, as well as a thematic thread for the question clusters created. Top-rung questions may be used as a journal prompt or as part of a graded open-ended writing response. Grades also could be given, based on guided discussion, after students are familiar with the processes and acceptable responses with evidence. Most of the higher level rung questions, products, and activities can be used for grading. Other rungs may be used that way as well, depending on the thinking required and the task demand.

Time Allotment

Although the time needed to complete Jacob's Ladder tasks will vary by student, most lessons should take students 15–30 minutes to read the selection aloud or with a partner and another 20–30 minutes to complete one ladder individually. More time is required for paired student and whole-group discussion of the questions or for specific creative synthesis tasks that involve more writing or researching. Teachers may wish to set aside 2–3 days each week for focusing on one Jacob's Ladder reading and commensurate ladders, especially when introducing the program. When first starting out with the program, teachers have reported reading and discussing two ladders, taking up to a week. As students become more familiar with the process, the timing will vary based on student groupings, the length of the text, the specific questions and products to be completed, the number of ladders used, and student interest in the topic. It is important in introducing the program to select a reading and follow-up ladder work that could be completed in a period in order to model what the program intends.

Alignment to Common Core State Standards in English Language Arts

The new Common Core State Standards are K–12 content standards, developed in math and language arts to illustrate the curriculum emphases needed to develop in all students the skills and concepts needed for the 21st century. Adopted or adapted by many states to date, the standards are organized into key content strands and articulated across all years of schooling. The initiative has been state-based and collaboratively led through two consortia and coordinated by the National Governors Association (NGA) and the Council of Chief State School Officers (CCSSO). Designed by teachers, administrators, and content experts, the standards seek to prepare K–12 students for college and the workplace.

The new standards in language arts are evidence-based, aligned with expectations for success in college and the workplace, and informed by the successes and failures of the current standards and international competition demands. They stress rigor, depth, clarity, and coherence, drawing from key national and international reports in mathematics and science. They provide a framework for curriculum development work that remains to be done—although many states are engaged in this ongoing process.

Alignment Approaches to the Jacob's Ladder Reading Comprehension Program

Jacob's Ladder exemplifies a model curriculum that addresses the Common Core State Standards in English language arts—with informational texts spanning all content areas—through several approaches, including advanced readings, the use of higher level skills and product demands that address the Common Core emphases for argument and persuasion directly, and a focus on concept/theme development that is mirrored in the new standards.

There are three major strategies the authors of Jacob's Ladder: Nonfiction have used to accomplish the alignment to the Common Core State Standards and advanced instruction that goes beyond typical standards expected of all students.

- Jacob's Ladder provides pathways to advance the learning of the Common Core State Standards for gifted learners. Some of the standards do address higher level skills and concepts that should receive focus throughout the years of schooling, such as a major emphasis on the skills of argument in language arts. However, there are also more discrete skills that may be clustered across grade levels and compressed around higher level skills and concepts for more efficient mastery by the gifted. The Jacob's Ladder curriculum series moves students from lower order comprehension skills in reading to higher order critical reading and thinking skills within the same set of activities, thus advancing their higher level learning in verbal areas.

- The program provides differentiated task demands to address specific Common Core State Standards, and these cut across multiple disciplines but are embedded within contextual analysis and understanding of informational texts across multiple disciplines.

- Standards, such as the reading information text standard in the new Common Core English language arts standards, lend themselves to differentiated interpretation by demonstrating what a typical learner might be able to do at a given stage of development versus what a gifted learner might be able to do (Hughes, Kettler, Shaunessy-Dedrick, & VanTassel-Baska, 2014; VanTassel-Baska, 2013). The differentiated ladder examples in Jacob's Ladder: Nonfiction also show greater complexity, depth, and creativity, using a more advanced curriculum base.

Teachers and administrators are encouraged to align their standards to the different rungs of Jacob's Ladder. This exercise allows educators to see visually which ladders may need more emphasis based on a curriculum standard, and also to see where the highest leveled rungs of Jacob's Ladder may not be emphasized as much for most learners. However, they are a necessary component for stretching student thinking and differentiating for those who are ready for higher level skills. A chart is included in Appendix C to identify the connections to the CCSS standards of the ladder selections in this book.

Because English language arts standards can be grouped together in application, much of the project work in Jacob's Ladder connects to the new Common Core State Standards and shows how multiple standards can be addressed across content areas. For example, research projects are designed to address the research standard in English language arts by delineating a product demand for research on an issue, beginning by asking researchable questions and using multiple sources to answer them, and then representing the findings in tables, graphs, and other visual displays that are explained in the text and presented to an audience with implications for a plan of action. This approach to interdisciplinary work across math, science, and fictional texts is a central part of the Jacob's Ladder: Nonfiction program.

References

Beck, I. L., & McKeown, M. G. (1998). Comprehension: The sine qua non of reading. In S. Patton & M. Holmes (Eds.), *The keys to literacy* (pp. 40–52). Washington, DC: Council for Basic Education.

Bransford, J. D., Brown, A. L., & Cocking, R. R. (2000). *How people learn: Brain, mind, experience.* Washington, DC: National Academy Press.

Brozo, W., Shiel, G., & Topping, K. (2007). Engagement in reading: Lessons learned from three PISA countries. *Journal of Adolescent and Adult Literacy, 51,* 304–315.

Calkins, L., Ehrenworth, M., & Lehman, C. (2012). *Pathways to the Common Core: Accelerating achievement.* Portsmouth, NH: Heinemann.

Chin, C. A., Anderson, R. C., & Waggoner, M. A. (2001). Patterns of discourse in two kinds of literature discussion. *Reading Research Quarterly, 30,* 378–411.

Duke, N. K., Bennett-Armistead, V. S., & Roberts, E. M. (2003). Filling the great void: Why we should bring nonfiction into the early-grade classroom. *American Educator, 27,* 30–35.

French, H. (2006). *The use of Jacob's Ladder to enhance critical thinking abilities in gifted and promising learner populations* (Unpublished doctoral dissertation). William & Mary, Williamsburg, VA.

Guthrie, J. T., Schafer, W. D., & Huang, C. (2001). Benefits of opportunity to read and balanced instruction on the NAEP. *Journal of Educational Research, 94,* 145–162.

Harvey, S. (2002). Nonfiction inquiry: Using real reading and writing to explore the world. *Language Arts, 80,* 12–22.

Hughes, C. E., Kettler, T., Shaunessy-Dedrick, E., & VanTassel-Baska, J. (2014). *A teacher's guide to using the Common Core State Standards with gifted and advanced learners in the English language arts.* Waco, TX: Prufrock Press.

Moss, B. (2005). Making a case and a place for effective content area literacy instruction in the elementary grades. *The Reading Teacher, 59,* 46–55.

Moss, B., & Hendershot, J. (2002). Exploring sixth graders' selection of nonfiction trade books. *The Reading Teacher, 56,* 6–17.

Pressley, M., Wharton-McDonald, R., Allington, R., Block, C. C., Morrow, L., Tracey, D., . . . Woo, D. (2001). A study of effective first-grade literacy instruction. *Scientific Studies of Reading, 5*, 35–58.

Rawson, K. A., Dunlosky, J., & Thiede, K. W. (2000). The rereading effect: Metacomprehension accuracy improves across reading trials. *Memory & Cognition, 28*(6), 1004.

Rogers, K. (2002). *Re-forming gifted education: How parents and teachers can match the program to the child*. Scottsdale, AZ: Great Potential Press.

Rogers, K. B. (2007). Lessons learned about educating the gifted and talented: A synthesis of the research on educational practice. *Gifted Child Quarterly, 51*, 382–396.

Stambaugh, T. (2007). *Effects of the Jacob's Ladder Reading Comprehension Program* (Unpublished doctoral dissertation). William & Mary, Williamsburg, VA.

Taylor, B. M., Pearson, P. D., Peterson, D. S., & Rodriguez, M. C. (2003). Reading growth in high-poverty classrooms: The influence of teacher practices that encourage cognitive engagement in literacy learning. *The Elementary School Journal, 104*, 3–30.

Taylor, B. M., Peterson, D. S., Pearson, P. D., & Rodriguez, M. C. (2002). Looking inside classrooms: Reflecting on the "how" as well as the "what" in effective reading instruction. *Reading Teacher, 56*, 270–279.

Tivnan, T., & Hemphill, L. (2005). Comparing four literacy reform models in high-poverty schools: Patterns of first-grade achievement. *Elementary School Journal, 105*, 419–443.

VanTassel-Baska, J. (2013). *Using the Common Core State Standards for English language arts with gifted and advanced learners*. Waco, TX: Prufrock Press.

VanTassel-Baska, J., & Stambaugh, T. (2006a). *Comprehensive curriculum for gifted learners* (3rd ed.). Needham Heights, MA: Allyn & Bacon.

VanTassel-Baska, J., & Stambaugh, T. (2006b). Project Athena: A pathway to advanced literacy development for children of poverty. *Gifted Child Today, 29*(2), 58–65.

VanTassel-Baska, J., & Little, C. (Eds.). (2017). *Content-based curriculum for gifted learners* (2nd ed.). Waco, TX: Prufrock Press.

Villaume, S. K., & Brabham, E. G. (2002). Comprehension instruction: Beyond strategies. *The Reading Teacher, 55*, 672–676.

Part II: Readings and Student Ladder Sets by Discipline

Section 1: Science 25
Section 2: Math 49
Section 3: Social Studies 65

SECTION 1

Science

Section 1 includes the selected readings and accompanying question sets for each science selection. Each reading is followed by up to two sets of questions; each set is aligned to one of the six ladder skills. The ladder skills covered by each selection are as follows:

Reading Titles	Ladders	Comparison Ladder
The Search for the Ninth Planet	D	
The Aerodynamics of Crickets	A	B
Bumblebee Watch	A	B
A Pox on You!	B, D	
In Tests of Mathematical Ability, Wolves Lead the Pack Over Dogs	D	
Grace Murray Hopper, Computer Scientist	A, B	

The Search for the Ninth Planet

According to a new study by scientists Konstantin Batygin and Mike Brown, there may be a ninth planet orbiting in the far reaches of our solar system. This isn't the first time the existence of a ninth planet has been discussed. But Batygin and Brown are the first to build a solid argument with calculations and data to support their position. They built upon a previous study from 2014, which noted oddities in the orbits of some objects beyond Neptune. Batygin and Brown researched these findings further and found that these oddities matched their calculations for a planet-sized object.

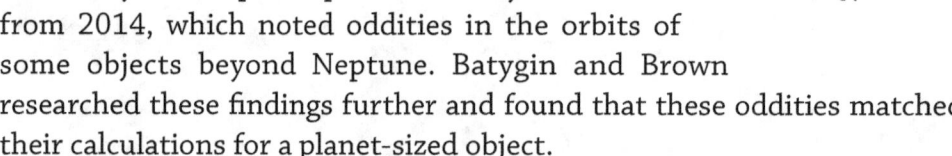

Although the scientists haven't actually seen the ninth planet, they have developed a strong case for its existence by looking at the clustering of other objects orbiting beyond Neptune. These objects aren't adhering to usual gravitational rules. According to Batygin and Brown, it's very unlikely that this clustering could be a coincidence. Instead, they believe that another, much larger planet is pulling those smaller objects into its own orbit. "Think of the planet as a dog that shepherds the six objects, like it would sheep," Batygin said.

Planet Nine would most likely be a rocky core covered in methane and nitrogen gas. It would be dim and difficult to see, which might explain why no one has spotted it yet. Planet Nine could be up to 10 times as massive as Earth, and would be located far beyond the Kuiper Belt, a region of small icy worlds beyond Neptune. In fact, the planet would come no closer to the sun than 30.5 billion km, a distance 5 times farther than Pluto. That means it could take Planet Nine 10,000–20,000 years to orbit the sun.

But how could a planet get so far from the sun? And why would it stay in that distant orbit rather than moving out of our system? Batygin and Brown have some theories. They propose that 4 billion years ago, the planets were packed so tightly in the inner solar system that they couldn't all develop. Consequently, Planet Nine was ejected. The gases present during that time slowed its movement so that it stayed in our solar system, settling into a distant orbit around the sun.

However exciting these discoveries may be, Batygin and Brown know that they need to actually find the planet before they can receive the full support of the scientific community. A few scientists are unconvinced, and hope that more research will support the case for Planet Nine. "Until there's a direct detection, it's a hypothesis—even a potentially very good hypothesis," Brown said.

Brown is excited to make this discovery. In 2005, his work led to Pluto's reclassification as a dwarf planet. "Killing Pluto was fun" he said, "but this is head and shoulders above everything else."

However, spotting a distant planet, even with the strongest telescopes on Earth, could take 5 or more years. For this reason, Batygin and Brown are opening the search to the larger community. Scientists are now using Subaru, an 8-meter telescope in Hawaii, to search for Planet Nine. With their combined efforts, we may soon have proof of our ninth planet.

References

Hand, E. (2016). Astronomers say a Neptune-sized planet lurks beyond Pluto. *Science*. Retrieved from http://www.sciencemag.org/news/2016/01/feature-astronomers-say-neptune-sized-planet-lurks-unseen-solar-system

Lemonick, M. D. (2016). Strong evidence suggests a super Earth lies beyond Pluto. *Scientific American*. Retrieved from http://www.scientificamerican.com/article/strong-evidence-suggests-a-super-earth-lies-beyond-pluto1

Stirone, S. (2016). The search for the real Planet X. *Popular Science*. Retrieved from http://www.popsci.com/search-for-real-planet-x

Name: _____ Date: _____

Creative Synthesis

D3

Research the criteria for a celestial body to become a planet. What would the scientists need to consider that wasn't already discussed in the article? Use the reference list as a starting place for your research.

Summarizing

D2

Why do scientists think they've found a ninth planet? What evidence do they have? Summarize their evidence in the following chart:

Evidence for a Ninth Planet	Where the Information Was Found in the Text
1.	
2.	
3.	

Paraphrasing

D1

Why are the scientists not able to see the planet yet?
Explain in your own words in a short paragraph.

The Aerodynamics of Crickets

Dr. Rajat Mittal of Johns Hopkins University was about to rid his basement of spider crickets when he noticed something fascinating about their movements; the crickets could jump astonishing distances and almost always landed on their feet. He decided to conduct a study with his students at the Whiting School of Engineering to gather data about the jumping and landing patterns of the small insects.

The spider cricket, sometimes called the camel cricket, can leap up to 60 times its body length. For a human, that would be the equivalent of jumping across an entire football field. The spider cricket also tends to touch down smoothly, no matter what kind of surface it lands on. This aerodynamic success makes it an excellent specimen to study. It may even provide data for the future development of small jumping robots.

Mittal and his students set up three high-speed video cameras to capture the hundreds of stages that crickets go through as they move through the air. They then slowed the video footage and studied the crickets' movements. "We're looking at the way the spider crickets move their bodies and move their limbs to stabilize their posture during a jump," said Emily Palmer, student at Johns Hopkins and lead researcher of Mittal's team. She and the others found that the crickets manipulated their legs and antennae to make their jumps more effective. The research team also used 3-D computer models to calculate the degree of wind drag on the spider crickets' limbs.

Mittal described the insects as masters of aerodynamics: "It's only when you slow these critters down that you really start to see the beauty and the intricacy of their movement. The analogy that comes to mind is of a ballerina performing a ballet. It's a very beautiful, controlled, intricate motion."

As the crickets take off, they streamline their bodies in order to cover more distance. Then, just at the peak of the jump, they move their legs away from their bodies in order to stabilize their descent at an angle of 55 to 60 degrees. By shifting the position of their legs, the crickets can set up the conditions needed for a perfect landing. Mittal compared the movement to a parachutist in free fall, but noted that the crickets' extra limbs and antennae made the movement even more effective. As the crickets descend, they maintain the same angle until they land, touching ground again on their back legs. "It's like an aircraft landing," Mittal said.

Name: _____   Date: _____

These findings could help scientists to develop a new generation of small jumping robots that could serve as mechanical helpers to humans. These micro robots could traverse rugged terrain and uneven ground, and might be used in areas where humans cannot move safely. Unlike previous robots, they could jump between earthbound and airborne states, rather than relying on just one or the other. For example, a jumping robot could move easily around earthquake rubble or the unfamiliar surface of a new planet.

Although Mittal and his team are not currently studying these practical applications, they hope that their findings will help future developers. This project could potentially continue for the next few years, with researchers testing the crickets in variable conditions and gathering more data on their movements. In this case, as in others, studying nature and its evolution may help humans in the near or distant future.

References

Gorman, J. (2015). Crickets and their spectacular dancelike leaps. *The New York Times*. Retrieved from http://www.nytimes.com/2015/11/02/science/crickets-and-their-spectacular-dancelike-leaps.html?_r=0

Pitts, J. (2015). Study of spider crickets a leap into aerodynamics. *The Baltimore Sun*. Retrieved from http://www.baltimoresun.com/health/bs-hs-cricket-robotics-20151209-story.html

Sneiderman, P. (2015). Researchers at Johns Hopkins study crickets' aerial acrobatics in hopes of building better robots. *HUB*. Retrieved from http://hub.jhu.edu/2015/10/20/spider-crickets-jumping-robotics

Name: _____ Date: _____

Consequences and Implications

A3

What are the implications of using animals in research? Is this a good idea? Write a persuasive essay explaining your ideas, using evidence from this article as well as at least three additional articles you find. Be sure to include specific evidence that supports your point of view and also explains why other points of view are not as viable. Prepare an outline for your essay, using the following chart:

Evidence for Use of Animals in Research		
Pro Arguments	**Con Arguments**	**Sources Used**

Cause and Effect

A2

What applications do Mittal and his team see for the research done on spider crickets? What effect might it have on perfecting robots? Why do you think this research is important?

Sequencing

A1

Outline the steps Dr. Mittal and his colleagues performed to study the spider crickets' movements.

Bumblebee Watch

A decline in the bumblebee population may have catastrophic effects across North America and Europe in the years to come. The roughly 250 bumblebee species in the genus *Bombus* are critical pollinators, meaning they are essential to the production of about a third of the food and drink humans consume. Berries, tree fruits, peppers, and tomatoes are among the crops that rely on bumblebees for pollination.

Although many kinds of bees are needed to encourage plant production, bumblebees are unique for many reasons: they are strong flyers, with wings that beat 130 times per second; they engage in "buzz pollination," vibrating against flowers in order to release large amounts of pollen; and, unlike other kinds of bees, their large bodies produce heat that allows them to pollinate early in the morning and late at night.

In the last few years, however, researchers were alarmed to find that four once-common species of *Bombus* have disappeared in North America. According to Sarina Jepsen, director of the Xerces Society for Invertebrate Conservation, "We've found that almost a third of North American bumblebee species are declining, and some are threatened with extinction." Many factors have contributed to this decline, including disease, unregulated trade, pesticides, habitat loss, and climate change.

One theory suggests that a nonnative parasitic fungus may have spread through bumblebee colonies in the 1990s. At the time, bumblebee queens were shipped to Europe to generate colonies there, and then shipped back to the United States. On their return trips, these bees may have brought the European disease with them.

Even though the U.S. suspended shipments of bees to Europe after the spread of the disease, trade of bumblebees continued to occur within the country. In fact, domestic trade has grown in the last two decades as consumption of berries and tomatoes has risen. More bees are shipped to new parts of the U.S. to generate increased output of crops. But transporting bees to nonnative areas can cause problems. If bees escape their colonies, they can affect the behaviors and populations of other insects and plants in the area.

Pesticides are another problem for the bumblebee population. A new class of long-lasting insecticides can result in bee deaths and decreased colony production. Researchers urge farmers to use pesticides only when necessary, and to take proper precautions when using them to limit the negative effects on bees.

Another study found that climate change is a huge factor in the decline of bumblebees. As the Earth grows warmer, many bumblebees in the southern areas of North America are not relocating to cooler areas in the north. The reasons for their refusal to move are not yet known. It is possible that the bees are unwilling to relocate because their native plants have not yet moved north. Scientists have considered moving the bees to a more suitable climate, but, as with bee trade, complications arise when introducing new species in unfamiliar areas.

Still, there is some good news from the bumblebee world. Recently, there has been a resurgence of *Bombus occidentalis*, a species common in the Pacific Northwest. These bees appeared to die out in the 1990s due to a parasite that spread through their hives, but many have been spotted in the area in 2016. Scientists are still unsure how these bees survived, but hope future research can aid in the conservation of other bees.

Experts are also encouraging the general public to join in bumblebee conservation efforts. Jeremy Kerr, a professor of biology at the University of Ottawa, hopes that people will react to the news of bee decline by encouraging climate reform: "Bees capture the public's imagination, and maybe that will help governments to act."

References

Mathewson, S. (2016). Rare bumblebee: Populations rebound in Pacific Northwest. *Nature World News*. Retrieved from http://www.natureworldnews.com/articles/19817/20160210/rare-bumblebee-populations-rebound-pacific-northwest.htm

Tangley, L. (2014). The buzz about bumblebees. *National Wildlife Federation*. Retrieved from https://www.nwf.org/News-and-Magazines/National-Wildlife/Gardening/Archives/2014/Bumblebees.aspx

Vaughan, A. (2015). Climate change causing bumblebee habitat loss, say scientists. *The Guardian*. Retrieved from http://www.theguardian.com/environment/2015/jul/09/bumblebee-habitat-shrinking-europe-north-america-climate-change-study

Name: _____ Date: _____

Consequences and Implications

A3

What might some of the unintended consequences be on humans, the environment, OR other animals if we followed all of the recommendations listed to save the bees? Use the following chart to help you organize your ideas.

Solution to Save or Protect the Bees	Consequences to Others

Cause and Effect

A2

What is the cause of the bee population decline? What effects might it have on humans and their future as a species?

Sequencing

A1

List all of the ways, according to the article, that bees are important to the environment. What would you say to someone who didn't like bumblebees, based on the information from this article?

BUMBLEBEE WATCH

Name: _____ Date: _____

Comparison Ladder for "The Aerodynamics of Crickets" and "Bumblebee Watch"

Animals are important to the environment and humans. The following ladder compares the article on bumblebees and the article on crickets to explore the importance of animals to research on the ecosystem.

35

Name: _____ Date: _____

COMPARISON LADDER FOR "THE AERODYNAMICS OF CRICKETS" AND "BUMBLEBEE WATCH"

Generalizations

B3

Write two generalizations about the importance of animals to humans and the environment. Support each statement with evidence from both articles.

Classifications

B2

Categorize your list from B1 about the importance of animals into no more than four categories. What are your categories and why did you choose them?

Details

B1

Based on the reading of both articles, how are animals important? Make a list.

A Pox on You!

In medieval times, there was no greater curse than to wish "a pox on you and your family." Smallpox was a horrible disease that covered the skin with pus-filled blisters and often killed its victims. Those who survived wore the scars for the rest of their lives. They had circular depressions covering their skin and disfiguring their faces. In severe cases, people lost parts of their lips and ears and the tips of their noses.

The first symptoms were fever, chills, headache, and backache. Then a rash covered the body and turned into pus-filled sores that made the skin feel like it was on fire. If the eyes were infected, they became cloudy and eventually all sight was lost. And most of the victims were children. It was a sickness that terrified parents because they knew that one in every three children who got smallpox died, and those who lived were scarred or blind.

European doctors were helpless to stop the disease. They tried making pastes from plants and feeding patients herbal teas. They hung red curtains around the bed of the patient hoping that the color red might take away the sickness. They even tried having the patient chew dried horse manure. Nothing helped. The one thing they did know was that people who recovered from smallpox never got the disease again, even if they nursed a person covered with smallpox sores. Once a person had smallpox, he or she was immune.

Doctors in the East were centuries ahead of European medicine. In 1000 CE, Chinese doctors had already discovered how to inoculate people against smallpox. They collected scabs from smallpox patients, ground them up, and blew the powder into the noses of healthy children. It was blown up the right nostril for a boy and up the left nostril for a girl. The child would become ill, but it was a much milder case of smallpox without the horrible scars and with little chance of death.

In India and the Arabic world, pus was collected from the sores of sick people. The physician then made a small cut in the skin of the healthy person and rubbed the pus into the slit. Within a few days, the person would be recovering from a mild case of smallpox and was immune for the rest of his life.

It wasn't until the 1700s that the British learned about inoculation. When Lord Montagu was named Ambassador to the Ottoman Empire, his wife attended a smallpox party in Constantinople. The amazed Lady Montagu wrote back to her friends that while she was at the party an old woman pulled from her skirts a nutshell filled with smallpox pus. The old woman asked who wanted the treatment, and adults and children held out their arms. She scratched them with a sharp needle and rubbed the pus into the wound.

Lady Montagu told her friends that the people suffered a mild form of the pox and were not scarred for life. Lady Montagu had contracted smallpox when she was 26 and her face was horribly scarred. She was convinced this was the way to spare her own children from scars and possible death. In 1717, she had her 6-year-old son take the treatment. It was successful, and when she returned to England, she had well-known surgeon Charles Maitland inoculate her 3-year-old daughter.

News of this new procedure spread quickly and soon surgeons throughout the British Empire were busy inoculating patients and experimenting with ways to improve the technique. One such scientist was Edward Jenner, who began experimenting with the milder illness cowpox in the 1790s.

He had observed that milkmaids who had suffered cowpox were also immune to smallpox. He began using cowpox as an inoculation ingredient. His experiments were quite successful because the patients had an even lower death and illness rate. The public was frightened about using a virus that came from cows, however. Cartoonists published pictures showing people growing horns and hooves because they took the cowpox inoculation.

But Jenner's vaccine was so good at preventing illness that it was accepted by both the medical community and the general public. By 1814, more than 3 million people in Europe had been vaccinated against smallpox. By the 1820s, smallpox vaccines were given around the world, and Edward Jenner was recognized as the hero who stopped smallpox.

Name: _____ Date: _____

FREAKY FACTS

Vaccine Fit for a Princess

In 1722, Princess Caroline of England wanted to have her daughters inoculated against smallpox, but she wanted to make sure that it was safe for the girls. So she promised six condemned felons that if they would test out the inoculation first they would receive a reprieve of their sentence—if they didn't die from the inoculation. All six survived, but Princess Caroline wanted more proof. Next, she forced 12 children attending a charity school to be inoculated. When all of them survived and had only mild cases of smallpox, then she allowed the princesses to receive the treatment.

FREAKY FACTS

Makeup Was Murder

In the 1700s, makeup was in style for both men and women. Paintings of the nobility show pale white faces with bright red cheeks. They also show tall white powdered wigs and elaborate hairstyles.

The white face powder was popular because it helped hide the deep pit-like scars that many people had from smallpox. The powder was made from very finely flaked lead and made a nice thick covering that hid the scars. Unfortunately the lead was highly poisonous and led to headaches, dizziness, and blindness. If the powder was accidentally ingested or eaten, it could lead to paralyzation or even death.

The red cheek rouge was not any better. Its ingredients included carmine, a lead-based pigment. The carmine was also used as lipstick, and it was next to impossible to avoid eating some of the lipstick. Many young ladies and gentlemen became gravely ill from the makeup they were using to hide their smallpox scars.

From *Twisted True Tales From Science: Medical Mayhem* by Stephanie Bearce, 2017, New York, NY: Taylor & Francis. Copyright 2017 by Taylor & Francis. Reprinted with permission.

Name: _____ Date: _____

Generalizations

B3

What additional true statements (i.e., generalizations) about inoculation besides "inoculation involves risk" can you make, based on this article and current-day practices? Write at least two more.

Classifications

B2

Research current-day inoculations that have worried people or seemed risky. How do your current findings compare to the smallpox inoculation explanation in the article? Categorize examples of diseases for which an inoculation might be successful.

Details

B1

What details in the article suggest that innovation involves risk?

A POX ON YOU!

Name: _____ Date: _____

Creative Synthesis

D3

What if you were someone in the 1800s getting a smallpox inoculation for the first time? Write a short journal article from that perspective, considering what that person might be thinking or feeling.

Summarizing

D2

Summarize the steps taken to prevent smallpox over time.

Paraphrasing

D1

What made doctors in the East (i.e., China and the Middle East) more successful at treating smallpox? Describe the methods they employed.

A POX ON YOU!

In Tests of Mathematical Abilities, Wolves Lead the Pack Over Dogs

You may think you have a smart dog at home, but when it comes to dogs and math, one set of researchers found that dogs don't quite add up when compared to the abilities of their biological ancestor, the wolf.

In 2012, researchers Friederike Range and Zsofia Virányi from the Messerli Research Institute at the University of Veterinary Medicine, Vienna showed that wolves can discriminate between quantities of food. A follow-up study, published in 2014, examined the same ability in dogs.

The animals, all raised at the Wolf Science Center in Austria and trained to take part in such cognition research projects, were tested with cheese cubes, dropped into opaque tubes. While the animal watched, an experimenter would extend his or her hand through a hole and drop some number of cheese cubes into a tube below the hole. The cubes always numbered between one and four pieces of cheese, and the experimenter held up his or her hand once the items were dropped. This procedure was repeated with a second tube, with some other number of cheese cubes (also between one and four) dropped on that side. The dog or wolf then was prompted to step on a buzzer to show which side contained more cheese cubes. If the animal chose correctly, the cubes would be released for the animal to eat.

When the wolves took their turn at the experiment, the wolves chose correctly between two and four cubes, three and four cubes, two and three cubes, and all other ratios of cubes. While not perfect, the wolves got the right answer more often than not. The dogs, however, were found to only get the right answer if one of the tubes had double the number of the other tube.

Various controls were put into place, including early tests to determine if the animals could work the testing machine, measures to make sure the animals couldn't receive cues or hints from the human experimenter's body language, and even tests to see if adding small stones into the mix changed the animals' ability to discriminate the number of cheese cubes dropped. Range also noted that the experimenters ensured that the animals were shown the pieces sequentially (not in piles, as it's believed that most animals can tell a bigger stack of food from a smaller one), making it so that the animals had to mentally represent the number of pieces dropped into each tube.

Even with these controls, the wolves picked the correct side most often. But the dogs? They failed, showing performance on par with simply guessing.

"Dogs are better able to discriminate the quantities of food when they can see them in their entirety," says Range. "But this requires no mental representation."

Range and her colleagues are now examining why dogs would do so poorly on the tests in comparison with wolves. One theory exists that dogs may have lost their ability to mentally represent quantities of items through their domestication by humans. As Range noted, dogs no longer have to seek out or provide their own food. They no longer face social pressures like determining whether an opposing group outnumbers their own or even the decision of where to sleep. Although dogs may have lost cognitive skills like counting, they did gain other social smarts, especially when it comes to human-dog interactions.

References

Preston, E. (2014). Dogs not great at math (wolves are better). *Discover*. Retrieved from http://blogs.discovermagazine.com/inkfish/2014/12/19/dogs-not-great-math-wolves-better/#.Vvq8Dcc5PbA

University of Veterinary Medicine, Vienna. (2014). A lot or a little? Wolves discriminate quantities better than dogs. *ScienceDaily*. Retrieved from http://www.sciencedaily.com/releases/2014/12/141216100527.htm

Name: _____ Date: _____

Creative Synthesis

D3

Think about what you know about how to conduct an experiment. Outline the processes that you understand are necessary to conduct research in the chart below. Describe each process briefly.

	Necessary Processes
Before the Experiment	
During the Experiment	
After the Experiment	

Summarizing

D2

Create a news headline for this article that is accurate yet "catchy," such that people would want to read it. Be ready to defend your headline.

Paraphrasing

D1

How do the researchers know that wolves are better at counting than dogs? Paraphrase their findings in your own words.

IN TESTS OF MATHEMATICAL ABILITIES, WOLVES LEAD THE PACK OVER DOGS

Grace Murray Hopper, Computer Scientist

Grace Hopper was one of the most influential computer scientists of the 20th century. Her work on computer languages paved the way for modern data processing as we know it.

Born on December 9, 1906, Grace always had a natural curiosity about the world around her. When she was 7, she took apart the alarm clocks in her home to see how they worked. She was fascinated with the inner lives of machines. Her parents encouraged her interest in education, and Grace went on to study math at Vassar College. From there, she attended Yale, where she pursued her master's degree, and in 1934, she received a Ph.D. in mathematics, a rare accomplishment at the time.

Armed with this education, Grace was fully equipped to work with the computers of her day. In the 1940s, computers were bulky machines that very few people knew how to program. At Harvard's Cruft Laboratory, Grace became the third person to program one of these computers—the Mark I, a 50-foot long machine that could solve long computations automatically. She worked on the Mark I, II, and III computers, developing difficult calculations to aid the U.S. Navy during the war. She is also credited with the terms *bug* and *debug* for an unlikely event that occurred during this project. While investigating a problem with the Mark II computer, her team found a moth stuck in the machine! She recorded the incident in their records as the "first actual case of bug being found."

In 1943, she joined the U.S. Naval Reserve. The navy had initially turned her down because of her age, but she was determined to help her country. After joining the reserves, she climbed quickly through the ranks and eventually became "Admiral" Grace Hopper.

This perseverance served her well in her academic and business ventures as well. Grace was a visionary, who could see what others couldn't. She realized the potential for computer processing; she knew that computers could be made available to a wider audience if coding became more user-friendly. The bulky machines that only a few scientists could program had the potential to become widely used and well understood by the average worker.

This vision of the future led her to accept a position at the Sperry Corporation as Senior Mathematician. There she worked on the first large-scale electronic digital computer. She and her team worked on improving computer code by developing COBOL, Common Business Oriented Language, one of the first programming languages. Eventually the team was able to translate symbolic code into machine code using the UNIVAC, a computer that recorded information on high-speed magnetic tape. For the first time, a computer was able to read text instead of just numbers!

Grace knew that the key to sharing computing with a wider audience was the development of programming languages. However, it was very difficult to convince others that computers could be made to "understand" English text. As far as most people knew, computers could only work with arithmetic. Grace had to use her persuasive skills to convince business managers to invest in computer languages. She was an excellent speaker, able to use images and analogies to help people understand how computers and computer languages worked. Soon, more and more businesses were using computers to aid them in bankroll and other automated services.

Grace also worked to standardize computer languages. Once computers and computer languages became more widely used, standards were needed to allow scientists to share and communicate data, both nationally and internationally.

When she finally retired at 80 years old, Admiral Grace Hopper was the oldest active duty officer in the United States. She won countless awards, including the National Medal of Technology and the Defense Distinguished Service Medal. When asked about her accomplishments, "Amazing Grace" Hopper felt that her greatest contribution was the impact she had on young computer scientists. That impact continues today with the Grace Hopper Celebration of Women in Computing, the largest technical conference for women.

References

Famous Women Inventors. (n.d.). *Dr. Grace Murray Hopper*. Retrieved from http://www.women-inventors.com/Dr-Grace-Murray-Hopper.asp

PBS. (1998). *People and discoveries: Grace Murray Hopper*. Retrieved from http://www.pbs.org/wgbh/aso/databank/entries/btmurr.html

School of Mathematics and Statistics, University of St. Andrews. (1999). *Grace Brewster Murray Hopper*. Retrieved from http://www-gap.dcs.st-and.ac.uk/~history/Biographies/Hopper.html

Yale University. (n.d.). *Grace Murray Hopper*. Retrieved from http://www.cs.yale.edu/homes/tap/Files/hopper-story.html

Name: _____ Date: _____

Consequences and Implications

A3

What were the implications of her work on the field of computer science?

Cause and Effect

A2

How did Grace do things differently from others? What qualities impacted her success?

Sequencing

A1

What was the sequence of events in Grace's early life that appeared to influence her later accomplishments?

GRACE MURRAY HOPPER, COMPUTER SCIENTIST

Name: _____ Date: _____

GRACE MURRAY HOPPER, COMPUTER SCIENTIST

Generalizations

B3

What generalizations might we draw about the following:
- the role of education in developing success in life?
- the role of perseverance in accomplishment?
- the role of being born into a particular family?
- the role of being female in an all-male profession?

Classifications

B2

Classify the abilities you have listed as related to her accomplishments. Which abilities served Grace well across her life?

Details

B1

What are examples of Grace's abilities in several areas?

SECTION 2

Math

Section 2 includes the selected readings and accompanying question sets for each math selection. Each reading is followed by up to two sets of questions; each set is aligned to one of the six ladder skills. The ladder skills covered by each selection are as follows:

Reading Titles	Ladders	Comparison Ladder
Making Math Fun	A, D	
An Introduction to Magic Squares	D	
Counting Like a Greek	C, D	
Should Students Use Calculators During Math?	A, D	

Making Math Fun

For much of the population, math can be difficult and even frustrating. But what if we could make math fun? More researchers and educators in the U.S. are promoting recreational math outside of school in order to boost students' interest in mathematics. If problems are fun to tackle, they say, then students will become more driven to learn and make discoveries. This increased interest can aid students in school and beyond.

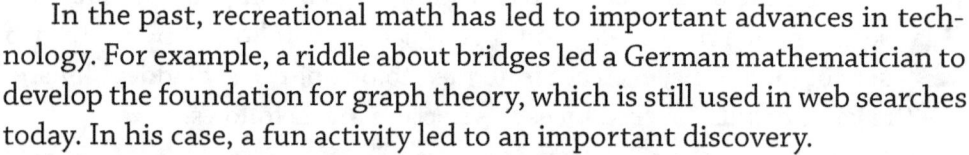

Recreational math includes any kind of logic or deduction problem that requires no advanced knowledge (meaning you won't need calculus or advanced geometry to find the answer). Recreational math puzzles should be fun, but should also lead to a moment of discovery, a flash of insight when all the pieces of a puzzle suddenly become clear.

In the past, recreational math has led to important advances in technology. For example, a riddle about bridges led a German mathematician to develop the foundation for graph theory, which is still used in web searches today. In his case, a fun activity led to an important discovery.

But how can we make math fun for those of use who aren't mathematicians? According to recent research, math anxiety is a huge problem in the U.S. However, this anxiety may stem from testing concerns and confidence issues rather than from an actual dislike of math. The pressure to perform well may be undermining students' interest in math in school. Outside of the classroom, in clubs and afterschool activities, students are more likely to engage in math for fun.

Another study pointed out that the Common Core State Standards, the educational initiative that details what American K–12 students should know, focuses mostly on results, or correct answers, rather than the mathematical process used by students. On the other hand, the standard curricula of other countries often emphasize process, using words like *enjoyment*, *curiosity*, *beauty*, and *value* when detailing students' experience.

Some schools and programs are hoping to move toward this personal experience of math. For example, some schools in Newark, NJ, tested out a new educational app for smartphones called "Bedtime Math." Parents were encouraged to have their children solve one puzzle or riddle a night. Kids found the app fun because their responses weren't graded or monitored; the process was voluntary and never considered "homework." As Laura Deck, creator of the app, said, "It's not pedagogy. It's playful."

Name: _____   Date: _____

The program had success in these early trials. The University of Chicago found that first graders who had engaged with "Bedtime Math" for a certain number of weeks outperformed first graders who had not.

Afterschool programs can also help kids develop an interest in math. One program, "Crazy8's," aims to help kids discover and nurture a love of numbers by presenting them with fun activities that involve math. During the club, kids learn by running, building, jumping, and making music. Math is presented as a hands-on activity, rather than as a complex page of numbers.

It will take time for schools to implement recreational math in the classroom. Teachers may have difficulty incorporating lessons that stray too far from the required material. In the meantime, students have options to pursue recreational math at home and at clubs. The key to success may be as simple as learning to enjoy learning.

References

Heitin, L. (2016). What we know about struggling math students, according to PISA results. *Education Week*. Retrieved from http://blogs.edweek.org/edweek/curriculum/2016/02/what_we_know_about_students_who_struggle_international_math_test.html

Herzog, L. (2016). Will kids do math for fun? Newark schools think new app will help. *NJ.com*. Retrieved from http://www.nj.com/essex/index.ssf/2016/02/newark_public_school_parents_are_using_a_new_app_t.html

Sumpter, L. (2015). Recreational mathematics—Only for fun? *Journal of Humanistic Mathematics, 5*(1), 121–138. DOI:10.5642/jhummath.201501.07. Retrieved from http://scholarship.claremont.edu/jhm/vol5/iss1/7

Suri, M. (2015). The importance of recreational math. *The New York Times*. Retrieved from http://www.nytimes.com/2015/10/12/opinion/the-importance-of-recreational-math.html?_r=0

Williamson, C. (2016). Program makes math fun, games. *Parsonssun.com*. Retrieved from http://www.parsonssun.com/news/article_53863f36-d07b-11e5-a462-e3f06843f99f.html

Name: _____ Date: _____

Consequences and Implications

A3

What are the positive and negative consequences that might arise in the future if schools followed the ideas in the article about making math recreational? Debate the following question as a class, using information from the article and your own ideas:

"Should students be required to do math games and puzzles outside of school?"

Cause and Effect

A2

What effect, according to the article, does the author suggest that recreational mathematics will have on students? On schools? On society?

Sequencing

A1

Why does the author propose making math recreational? Highlight all of the reasons in order of importance from highest to least. Be ready to justify your opinion.

Name: _____ Date: _____

Creative Synthesis

D3

Create a 60-second television ad OR advertisement poster that uses information from the article, other articles, and your own ideas to support doing schoolwork outside of the classroom as a way to (a) help kids love a subject area or (b) reduce anxiety in a school. Make sure your information appeals to a variety of audiences and provides evidence.

Summarizing

D2

What solutions does the article suggest to get students to like math or feel less anxious about it? Do you agree or disagree with these solutions? Why or why not?

Paraphrasing

D1

Why do some students hate math or feel anxious about it, according to the article? Provide at least three reasons with evidence. How do you feel about math and what are your reasons?

An Introduction to Magic Squares
by NRICH team

8	1	6
3	5	7
4	9	2

Magic Squares are square grids with a special arrangement of numbers in them. These numbers are special because every row, column, and diagonal adds up to the same number. So for the example to the left, 15 is the magic number. Could you work this out just from knowing that the square uses the numbers from 1 to 9?

Also, the two numbers that are opposite each other across the center number will add up to the same number. So in the square above, 8 + 2 = 10, 6 + 4 = 10, 1 + 9 = 10, and 3 + 7 = 10. Why is this?

The "order" of a magic square tells how many rows or columns it has. So a square with 3 rows and columns is Order 3, and a square with 4 rows and columns is Order 4 and so on.

So the numbers in the Magic Square are special, but why are they called magic? It seems that from ancient times they were connected with the supernatural and magical world. The earliest record of magic squares is from China in about 2200 BC, and is called "Lo-Shu." There's a legend that says that the Emperor Yu saw this magic square on the back of a divine tortoise in the Yellow River.

The black knots show even numbers and the white knots show odd numbers. Look closely and you'll see that this ancient magic square is the same as our example above. Magic squares were first mentioned in the Western world in the work of Theon of Smyrna. They were also used by Arab astrologers in the 9th century to help work out horoscopes. The work of the Greek mathematician Moschopoulos in 1300 AD help to spread knowledge about magic squares. So here we are now, more than 700 years later, and teachers are using them in class for problem solving and practicing addition.

You can make similar magic squares, of Order 3, using different numbers. Can you see any patterns in the numbers that work?

Note. From "An Introduction to Magic Squares" by NRICH team, 2011, retrieved from http://nrich.maths.org/2476. Copyright 2011 by NRICH (http://www.nrich.maths.org). Reprinted with permission.

Name: _____ Date: _____

Creative Synthesis

D3

Create your own magic square based on examples from the article. Ask a friend to solve it.

Summarizing

D2

In your own words, explain how a magic square works, based on information from the article.

Paraphrasing

D1

Why are magic squares called "magic"?

Name: _____ Date: _____

Counting Like a Greek

The Greek number system assigned numerical values to the letters of the alphabet. They used the 24 letters of the Greek alphabet plus three additional characters that are now obsolete (numbers 6, 90, and 900: digamma, koppa, and sampi—respectively) to denote numbers. The first nine letters of their early alphabet represented the numerals 1–9. The next nine letters represented multiples of 10, from 10 to 90. The next nine letters represented multiples of 100, from 100 to 900. At first, capital letters were used. Later they used lowercase letters. The Greek numerals up to 999 were quite easy to read if you knew all the symbols. However, 27 symbols were a lot to remember.

A	alpa	1	I	iota	10	P	rho	100
B	beta	2	K	kappa	20	Σ	sigma	200
Γ	gamma	3	Λ	lambda	30	T	tau	300
Δ	delta	4	M	mu	40	Y	upsilon	400
E	epsilon	5	N	nu	50	Φ	phi	500
F	digamma	6	Ξ	xi	60	X	chi	600
Z	zeta	7	O	omnicron	70	Ψ	psi	700
H	eta	8	Π	pi	80	Ω	omega	800
Θ	theta	9	ϟ	koppa	90	ϡ	sampi	900

To write numbers, the Greek simply combined the symbols from the chart and added the values for each symbol. Here are some examples:

$$NB = 50 + 2 = 52$$
$$ΨIH = 700 + 10 + 8 = 718$$
$$XΘ = 600 + 9 = 609$$
$$ΣNΔ = 200 + 50 + 4 = 254$$

Read these Greek numerals and write their value in our number system:

Θ = _____

ΞH = _____

PNE = _____

Name: _____   Date: _____

One problem with the Greek's system was that some numerals also spelled words. This could sometimes be confusing. It also led to superstitions about numbers that people associated with initials or with words they spelled. As you will see with the next problems, it might be hard to tell if a Greek was writing a word or a numeral.

Write the following numbers/letters in Greek using the chart to help you.

45 _____
375 _____
41 _____

It may seem like the Greeks had place value since they had symbols for hundreds, tens, and ones. However, it was the symbol that represented hundreds, not its placement. For example, Σ = 200, whether it stood alone or with other symbols. You could write ΣΜ or ΜΣ, ΣΕ or ΕΣ. The placement of Σ in the number did not change its value. It was always equal to 200.

When the Greeks wanted to write numerals in the thousands, they used the symbols for 1–9 followed by a "prime" sign ('). This meant that the number was multiplied by 1,000. For example:

A' = 1,000   B' = 2,000   Γ'ΝΖ = 3,057
(1 × 1000)   (2 × 1000)   (3 × 1,000) + 50 + 7

Refer to the chart of Greek numerals and write these Greek numerals in our number system.

Δ' _____
Ζ'ΠΔ _____
Β'Σ _____

For the ten thousands, Greeks used the capital M with other symbols. They wrote the M with another symbol written above it. The number on top of the M told how many 10,000's. Using the M to multiply numbers by 10,000 yielded the following numerals:

$\overset{A}{M}$ = 10,000 $\overset{E}{M}$Z' = 57,000 $\overset{Z}{M}$T = 70,300

57

Name: _____ Date: _____

Write these Greek numerals in our number system:

    E   B   Z

  MT = _____   M = _____   MOZ = _____

Now that you know more about the Greek number system, what new questions do you have?

Note. Adapted from *Can You Count in Greek?: Exploring Ancient Number Systems* by J. Leimbach & K. Leimbach (pp. 31–36), 2005, New York, NY: Taylor & Francis. Copyright 2005 by Taylor & Francis. Adapted with permission.

Name: _____ Date: _____

Theme/Concept

C3 Write a true statement about number systems, based on what you know about the Greek system and our Base 10 system.

Inference

C2 Compare and contrast the Greek number system with our current Base 10 number system. What are the similarities and differences? Create a Venn diagram to show your thinking.

Textual Elements and Understanding

C1 What are some of the important features of the Greek number system? Make a list, based on the article.

COUNTING LIKE A GREEK

Name: _____ Date: _____

Creative Synthesis

D3

Research **one** of the following questions and create an infographic that answers your question and provides evidence.
- Is the same Greek number system described in the article still used today? Why or why not?
- Why are digamma (6) koppa (90) and sampi (900) now obsolete?
- Create your own question of interest about the Greek number system.

Summarizing

D2

Answer the problems in the story and explain why your answers are correct, based on the information provided.

Paraphrasing

D1

Explain in your own words how place value differed in the Greek system, compared to our own Base 10 system. Provide an example to illustrate your thinking.

COUNTING LIKE A GREEK

Name: _____ Date: _____

Should Students Use Calculators During Math?

Educators continue to debate: Should calculators be frequently used in elementary math classrooms? The opinion among teachers and researchers is mixed. Since 1991, professional standards have recommended that teachers include calculators in the classroom at every grade level. Those who support calculators being used in the classroom often claim that they allow for accelerated and improved learning, in addition to increasing students' enjoyment of math. However, others consider calculators' use to prevent the deeper understanding of underlying mathematical concepts. Students may be at increased risk for relying too heavily on calculators to do the thinking for them. These two points of view represent opposing, but valid concerns for student learning when students use calculators in the classroom regularly.

Supporters of calculators in the classroom consider calculators to complement students' understanding of mathematics. Some argue that using calculators increases students' familiarity with technology while aiding their completion of math problems. For example, when engaged in math problems, calculators can be used as tools to check student work. Calculators provide needed accuracy and rapid feedback during student practice. In addition, teachers' focus can shift from problem repetition to understanding of math concepts. Students may also be better able to grasp the most efficient or prudent ways to solve problems by using calculators, as long as students already have a basic understanding of the math facts. Next, students may feel more confident in their own skills with more exposure to calculators in the classroom. Students can tackle more challenging problems that might be a step beyond their capabilities without using a calculator. Finally, for students who dislike math or find it boring, calculators can make math more fun and less dull.

Others claim that using calculators in the classroom is detrimental to students and their math abilities. One important concern is that students may rely on calculators too much, which may extend to not being able to perform simple math without a calculator's help. This is especially significant when students are not knowledgeable about math facts and cannot perform them by hand. Students may even develop a sense of false confidence in their own math skills. Next, calculators may hinder the use of logic to solve problems as well as students' deeper understanding of mathematical concepts. This can include selecting which problem-solving method is the best fit for the task at hand instead of trying out different options. Additionally, teachers worry that students may be able to cheat using notes stored on calculators, such as graphing calculators. A potential solution could be to implement a policy for when and where calculators can be used in the classroom. Finally, calculators are expensive, and every student and classroom might not have access to the same resources.

In conclusion, using calculators in the classroom to enhance learning has potential benefits and consequences. Although some may find calculators helpful to student learning, others believe that students may not fully develop necessary math skills as a result of using a calculator too often. Teachers may combat these negative effects by creating calculator policies, as well as requiring students to do some practice problems without a calculator. Although the answer of whether elementary math classrooms should use calculators is not yet clear, teachers and educators may weigh the benefits and costs to choose what to do in their own classrooms.

References

Concordia Online. (2016). *Pros and cons of allowing kids to use calculators in math class.* Retrieved from http://education.cu-portland.edu/blog/classroom-resources/pros-and-cons-of-allowing-kids-to-use-calculators-in-math-class

Moran, M. (2008). Calculators okay in math class, if students know the facts first. *Research News at Vanderbilt.* Retrieved from http://news.vanderbilt.edu/2008/08/calculators-okay-in-math-class-if-students-know-the-facts-first-62879

Starr, L. (2002). Educators battle over calculator use: Both sides claim casualties. *Education World.* Retrieved from http://www.educationworld.com/a_curr/curr072.shtml

Name: _____ Date: _____

Consequences and Implications

According to the article, what are the positive and negative implications on student learning of math when allowing students to use calculators? Use the chart below to help you organize your ideas:

Positive Implications of Using Calculators	Negative Implications of Using Calculators

A3

Cause and Effect

What are some of the effects of using calculators that have teachers concerned?

A2

Sequencing

Outline the key points of the argument on whether or not teachers should allow students to use calculators.

A1

SHOULD STUDENTS USE CALCULATORS DURING MATH?

Name: _____ Date: _____

Creative Synthesis

D3

Should students be permitted to use calculators in math? Determine your own point of view and argue for it by writing a persuasive essay. Remember to acknowledge multiple points of view.

Summarizing

D2

Are there conditions when using a calculator is okay versus times when it is less appropriate? Explain your thinking, using evidence from the article.

Paraphrasing

D1

Consider the following stakeholders and explain their position on using calculators for math. Use evidence from the article to help you come up with ideas as to what these individuals might say:
- Students
- Parents
- Teachers
- Mathematicians

SHOULD STUDENTS USE CALCULATORS DURING MATH?

SECTION 3

Social Studies

Section 3 includes the selected readings and accompanying question sets for each social studies selection. Each reading is followed by up to two sets of questions; each set is aligned to one of the six ladder skills.

The ladder skills covered by each selection are as follows:

Reading Titles	Ladders	Comparison Ladder
Surrender Speech	C	D
The Fight for the Nez Perce Indian Territory	A	D
The Struggles of Young Factory Workers in the Industrial Revolution	A	
Propaganda Posters and World War II	B, C	B
With God's Help, We Shall Prevail	C	B
Above and Beyond: Doris "Dorie" Miller and Pearl Harbor	C	
A New Kind of Snow Day for Students	A, C	
Should Students Be Required to Wear School Uniforms?	A, D	

Surrender Speech
Chief Joseph of the Nez Perce, 1877

Tell General Howard I know his heart. What he told me before, I have it in my heart. I am tired of fighting. Our chiefs are killed; Looking Glass is dead, Too-hul-hul-sote is dead. The old men are all dead. It is the young men who say yes or no. He who led on the young men is dead. It is cold, and we have no blankets; the little children are freezing to death. My people, some of them, have run away to the hills, and have no blankets, no food. No one knows where they are—perhaps freezing to death. I want to have time to look for my children, and see how many of them I can find. Maybe I shall find them among the dead. Hear me, my chiefs! I am tired; my heart is sick and sad. From where the sun now stands, I will fight no more forever.

Note. From "Surrender speech" by Chief Joseph of the Nez Perce, 1877, retrieved from http://etc.usf.edu/lit2go/185/civil-rights-and-conflict-in-the-united-states-selected-speeches/4856/the-surrender-of-chief-joseph-of-the-nez-perce-montana-territory-october-5-1877-chief-josephs-own-story. Reprinted from the public domain.

Name: _____ Date: _____

Theme/Concept

C3

What is the theme of this speech? How do you know?

Inference

C2

Why did Indian Chief Joseph give up? What inferences do you draw from his speech?

Textual Elements and Understanding

C1

What words or phrases are important to understanding this speech and how Chief Joseph feels?

SURRENDER SPEECH

The Fight for the Nez Perce Indian Territory

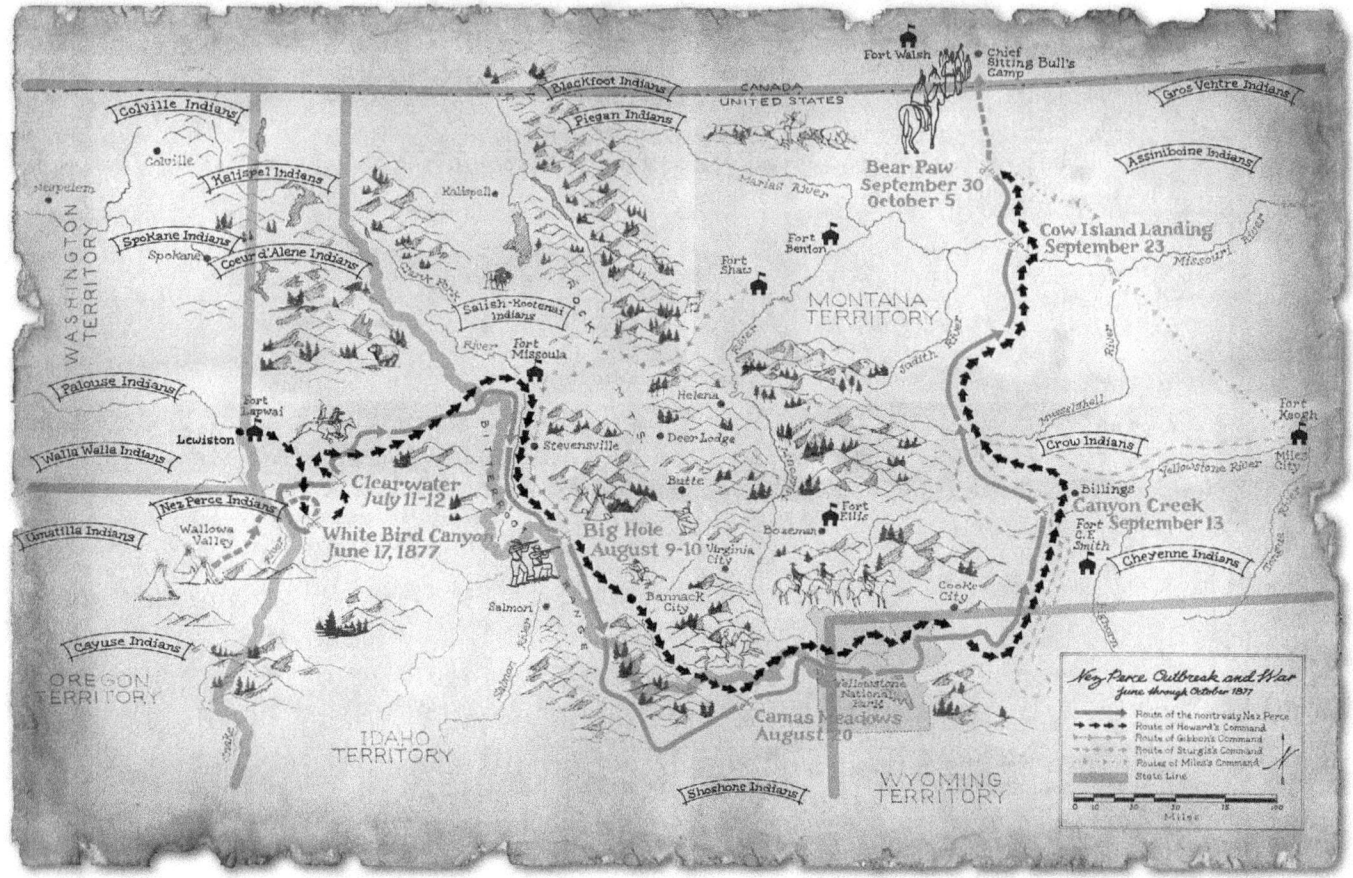

In 1877, war broke out between the Nez Perce, a Native American tribe, and the U.S. Army. Tensions between the two groups had been rising for the last few decades, but when the fighting finally broke out, both sides were surprised by the results.

The Nez Perce occupied the Wallowa Valley, and their land coved 17 million acres across modern-day Washington, Oregon, and Idaho. Their interactions with White settlers were originally peaceful; the Nez Perce helped guide Lewis and Clark on their famous expedition and even helped the U.S. to set up the Nez Perce reservation. However, after a gold rush in 1863, the government took back much of the land, leaving the Nez Pearce territory only a tenth of its original size. At the same time, U.S. leaders began to push the tribe to relocate to a different reservation in Idaho that was much smaller.

Nez Perce leader Chief Joseph resisted these relocation efforts during the early 1870s, but in 1877, General Oliver Otis Howard threated an attack on the tribe. In response, 20 young Nez Perce warriors staged a raid of White settlements, killing several people there. At this point, war was inevitable. Although Joseph had pushed for peace, he reluctantly left with the Nez Perce for Idaho.

What followed was one of the most impressive retreats in U.S. history. The Nez Perce had just 700 people in their party, and only 200 of them were warriors (with little formal training). The U.S. Army, on the other hand, had more than 2,000 soldiers, many of whom had fought in the Civil War. Still, the Nez Perce led an imposing force against the Army. Guided by Chief Looking Glass and Chief White Bird, their fighting skills and military tactics allowed them to avoid defeat for several months and even secure major victories. The tribe continued to move toward Idaho and Canada during the fall. But dwindling supplies, long miles of rough terrain, and the approaching winter weakened them and slowed their progress.

On October 5, 1877, after months of travel and evading the U.S. forces led by four different generals, Chief Joseph surrendered to General Nelson A. Miles and General Howard at Bear Paw Mountain. His surrender speech is still quoted today. Joseph's words at the conclusion of the war expressed a weariness of spirit that many Native Americans felt at that time. So many deaths had resulted from the war that it was difficult for Joseph to remain hopeful.

After the surrender, U.S. forces at first promised to see the Nez Perce home safely, but government plans changed. Chief Joseph and his tribe were sent to reservations in Kansas and Oklahoma. Although Joseph continued to work for the rights of his people—even meeting with President Rutherford B. Hayes to plead his case—the Nez Perce were not able to return to their home until 1885. Once they arrived, they were split up, with half of the tribe (including Joseph) relocated to a different reservation and land area that was much smaller than what they originally claimed.

Chief Joseph and the Nez Perce made a valiant stand for freedom. Joseph continued to speak against injustice for the rest of his life.

References

Kennaly, D. (2009). *The Nez Perce War of 1877*. Retrieved from https://www.army.mil/article/28124/The_Nez_Perce_War_of_1877

PBS. (n.d.). *The West—Chief Joseph*. Retrieved from http://www.pbs.org/weta/thewest/people/a_c/chiefjoseph.htm

Name: _____ Date: _____

Consequences and Implications

A3

What were the final consequences for Chief Joseph and the Nez Perce? For the U.S. government?

Cause and Effect

A2

Summarize the strategy of the generals as they worked to capture Chief Joseph and his tribe, based on information from the map. What made this battle one of the most impressive retreats in history? (Use the information from the map and the information from the article to explain your response.)

Sequencing

A1

Why were the U.S. government and the Nez Perce tribe fighting?

THE FIGHT FOR THE NEZ PERCE INDIAN TERRITORY

Name: _____ Date: _____

Comparison Ladder for "Surrender Speech" and "The Fight for the Nez Perce Indian Territory"

Chief Joseph's speech is compared to an explanation of the Nez Perce battle and a map of the paths taken by Chief Joseph and four different generals and their troops. The use of the map and explanation of the battles will help students understand the bravery and exhaustion of Chief Joseph and his tribe.

Name: _____ Date: _____

COMPARISON LADDER FOR "SURRENDER SPEECH" AND "THE FIGHT FOR THE NEZ PERCE INDIAN TERRITORY"

Creative Synthesis

D3

Why do you think Chief Joseph specifically said he has General Howard's words in his heart? Find more information about General Howard and Chief Joseph's relationship. Create a timeline or graphic that shows the history of the relationship between the two and the significance of the battle.

Summarizing

D2

How did the use of the map and explanation of the war help you better understand Chief Joseph's speech? Why might Chief Joseph say he was tired?

Paraphrasing

D1

Explain the purpose for the battle, in your own words, using evidence from both sources.

The Struggles of Young Factory Workers in the Industrial Revolution

Agnes Nestor, 1914. Reprinted from the public domain.

Agnes Nestor was born in Grand Rapids, MI, but moved with her family to Chicago at the age of 7. As a young teen, she went to work in a glove factory. By the age of 17, she was a veteran employee and a leading activist in the 10-day strike held at that glove factory in 1898. Nestor went on to become a famous labor organizer and activist. She was founder and first president of the International Glove Workers Union and president of the Women's Trade Union League. She was also instrumental in passing a 10-hour workday limit for women in Illinois. Below, she describes the conditions in the glove factory that caused her to join the 10-day strike in 1898.

Our machines were on long tables in large rooms, and we operators sat on both sides of the tables. At last I was where I had longed to be, and here I worked for ten years. I was earning fairly good pay for those times, and I was happy. We would mark out the quantity of our work and keep account of our earnings. I still have that little book in which I kept my accounts. It is interesting to see how I gradually increased my weekly pay.

To drown the monotony of work, we used to sing. This was allowed because the foreman could see that the rhythm kept us going at high speed. We sang "Bicycle Built for Two" and other popular songs.

Before we began to sing we used to talk very loudly so as to be heard above the roar of the machines. We knew we must not stop our work just to hear what someone was saying; to stop work even for a minute meant a reduction in pay.

. . . Also, there were some unjust practices, outgrowths from another era, which nettled us because they whittled away at our weekly pay. We were charged fifty cents a week for the power furnished our machines. At first we were tolerant of the charge and called it "our machine rent." But after a time that check-off of fifty cents from our weekly pay made us indignant.

We were obliged, besides, to buy our own needles. If you broke one, you were charged for a new one to replace it. We had, also, to buy our own machine oil. It was expensive; and to make matters worse, we had to go to certain out-of-the-way places to obtain it.

The glove-cutters, all men, had a union which had existed for about a year. The girl who sat next to me told me about it. She had a boyfriend in this union, but she was always careful not to let anyone hear her talk about it because in those days unions were taboo. She said that the cutters—all men—had talked of trying to get the girls to join the union and had wanted to approach our plant to suggest it, but that some of the members had said, "You'll never get those girls to join a union. They'll stand for anything up there!"

Israel Solon was one of these men. Sometimes, if a girl hesitated about going to the hall, he would urge: "Don't be afraid of the boss; protect yourself! Go to the union meeting!"

I went without hesitation. The meeting was a great success; workers packed the hall, and many non-members signed for membership. The work of organizing continued for three evenings, until most of the shop had been persuaded to join.

At the meeting we were called upon to state our demands. We gave them: no more machine rent; no paying for needles; free machine oil; union shop; raises for the cutters who were paid the lowest wages. . . .

. . . All this was happening at the same time that streetcar conductors were being discharged because it became known that they were forming a union. Some of the conductors, as they passed our picket line, would throw us handfuls of buttons which read: ORGANIZE. I'M WITH YOU!

We wore those buttons on our coats, and when we boarded the cars we would watch the expression on each conductor's face to find out whether or not he had joined the union. . .

Note. From *Engaging With History in the Classroom: The Post-Reconstruction Era* (pp. 189 & 192) by J. I. Robbins and C. L. Tieso, 2015, New York, NY: Taylor & Francis. Reprinted with permission.

Lilly O'Sullivan, a frail 13 year old girl working in the Drayton Mills, Spartenberg [sic], S.C. Been working four years, weaving, spinning, etc. Ran from 4 to 6 looms. Gets $3 a week. Location: Spartanburg, South Carolina. Photograph by Lewis Wickes Hine, 1912. Reprinted from the public domain.

Flossie Britt, 6 years old has been working several months steadily as spinner in the Lumberton Cotton Mills. Makes 30 cents a day. Lonnie Britt, 7 years old has been working steadily for 1 year as spinner. Makes 40 cents a day. Ages and data given me by their grandmother at home, and I saw them going and coming early and late. 2 smallest in the group. When Mr. Swift made his last visit to Lumberton he was shown through these mills by Mr. Jennings, who asked Mr. Swift how many children he thought there were under age. Mr. Swift said about 20, Mr. Jennings told him there were at least 30, and called one of his men to prove he was right. He told Mr. Swift that all the mills were employing children under age. Photograph by Lewis Wickes Hine, 1914. Reprinted from the public domain.

Name: _____ Date: _____

Consequences and Implications

A3

Write two generalizations about the implications of the Industrial Revolution on children, based on the account and photos provided.

Cause and Effect

A2

What inferences can you make about the causes and the effects of trying to unionize during the Industrial Revolution? Use the photos and the writings to develop the chart below.

Causes	Possible Effects of Actions Taken

Sequencing

A1

What details in the photos and Agnes Nestor's explanation of working conditions suggest that actions needed to be taken to make conditions better for the workers? List the details you notice and sequence them in order of importance from high to low.

THE STRUGGLES OF YOUNG FACTORY WORKERS IN THE INDUSTRIAL REVOLUTION

Propaganda Posters and World War II

"He gives 100%, you can lend 10%: Buy war stamps & bonds" by John McCrady, 1943. Created for Work Projects Administration War Services. Reprinted from the public domain.

"These colors won't run. Remember Pearl Harbor" by U.S. Office for Emergency Management War Production Board, ca. 1942–1943. Reprinted from the public domain.

Name: _____ Date: _____

"Non-stop work will win" by U.S. Office for Emergency Management, Office of War Infomration, ca. 1942-1945. Reprinted from the public domain.

"Scrap" by U.S. Office for Emergency Management, Office of War Infomration, ca. 1942-1945. Reprinted from the public domain.

Name: _____ Date: _____

"Soldiers without guns" by U.S. Office for Emergency Management, Office of War Information, ca. 1942–1945. Reprinted from the public domain.

"The Navy needs ships to avenge Pearl Harbor" by U.S. Office for Emergency Management, Office of War Information, ca. 1942–1945. Reprinted from the public domain.

"Your wartime duty! Don't waste water. Do not let water run a long time to get a drink. Do keep water in icebox instead" by Earl Kerkam, 1941–1943. Created for New York City Work Projects Administration War Services. Reprinted from the public domain.

During World War II, the American government and private sector turned to posters to help rally the public to get behind efforts to support the war overseas. Posters were ideal for making victory part of every citizen's personal mission, in part because people could encounter posters in a variety of places that other media couldn't reach, such as within schools, factories, stores, and offices. As noted by the National Museum of American History, posters "had democratic appeal—they could be made by anyone; they could be seen by all. Both medium and message spoke of democracy, which made posters ideal for expressing American war aims: why we fight, what we fight for" (para. 2).

War posters served a key element in the U.S. propaganda effort to mobilize the homefront. The posters promoted positive images of traditional middle class values such as family, patriotism, and free enterprise and sent a message that the home and factory could also serve as battlefields. Many posters worked to increase people's views of the responsibilities they could take on during war, whether it was salvaging metal, conserving water, buying war bonds and stamps, or planting victory gardens.

In addition to promoting the need for Americans to contribute at home, war posters often included stereotyped and exaggerated imagery of the enemy, suggesting that the enemy was not just a foe on the battlefield but representative of evil.

Posters were created by the Works Project Administration's (WPA) War Services project, which employed artists to create government materials. The Office of War Information (OWI), created in June 1942, was also responsible for overseeing (among many other duties) the creation and distribution of such posters. As noted by Bird and Rubenstein, the OWI had six categories of war information "themes"—many of which show up in posters of this era. They were:

- The Nature of the Enemy (detailed or general descriptions of the enemy, often negative such as what they hate or acts against others),
- The Nature of Our Allies (promoting ties with other nations),
- The Need to Work (how Americans must help to win the war),
- The Need to Fight (the need for war with weapons, bombs, and bare hands in order to win),
- The Need to Sacrifice (that Americans must give up luxuries and spare time to help win the war),
- The Americans (what we were fighting for, namely freedom, democracy, and "an end to discrimination against races and religions." (Bird & Rubenstein, p. 2)

References

Bird, W. L., Jr., & Rubenstein, H. (2013). Every citizen a soldier: World War II posters on the American home front. *History Now, 14.* Retrieved from https://www.gilderlehrman.org/sites/default/files/inline-pdfs/Every%20Citizen%20a%20Soldier%20Essay%20%28abridged%29.pdf

Maryland State Archives. (2004). *Depicting the enemy: Stereotype imagery in World War II.* Retrieved from http://teaching.msa.maryland.gov/000001/000000/000110/html/t110.html

National Museum of American History. (n.d.). *The poster's place in wartime.* Retrieved from http://americanhistory.si.edu/victory/victory2.htm

Name: _____ Date: _____

Generalizations

B3

What generalizations can you make about the need for patriotism during WWII?

Classifications

B2

Categorize the different posters listed. What message does each convey? Sort the posters and create your own categories. How do your categories match with the OWI categories explained in the article?

Details

B1

Look at the posters. What details do they have in common?

Name: _____ Date: _____

Theme/Concept

C3

If the government were creating posters today to garner American support for a cause, what would the cause be? Why? Create your own poster to garner support for something you believe in, using the same theme as the WWII posters.

Inference

C2

Why did the government need support from Americans and invest so much time in creating War posters?

Textual Elements and Understanding

C1

What purposes did the posters serve during WWII, according to the article?

PROPAGANDA POSTERS AND WORLD WAR II

With God's Help, We Shall Prevail

King George VI, First Radio Address, September 3, 1939

In this grave hour, perhaps the most fateful in our history, I send to every household of my peoples, both at home and overseas, this message, spoken with the same depth of feeling for each one of you as if I were able to cross your threshold and speak to you myself.

For the second time in the lives of most of us we are at war.

Over and over again we have tried to find a peaceful way out of the differences between ourselves and those who are now our enemies. But it has been in vain. We have been forced into a conflict. For we are called, with our allies, to meet the challenge of a principle which, if it were to prevail, would be fatal to any civilized order in the world. It is the principle which permits a state, in the selfish pursuit of power, to disregard its treaties and its solemn pledges; which sanctions the use of force, or threat of force, against the sovereignty and independence of other states. Such a principle, stripped of all disguise, is surely the mere primitive doctrine that "might is right"; and if this principle were established throughout the world, the freedom of our own country and of the whole of the British Commonwealth of Nations would be in danger. But far more than this—the peoples of the world would be kept in the bondage of fear, and all hopes of settled peace and of the security of justice and liberty among nations would be ended. This is the ultimate issue which confronts us. For the sake of all that we ourselves hold dear, and of the world order and peace, it is unthinkable that we should refuse to meet the challenge. It is to this high purpose that I now call my people at home and my peoples across the seas, who will make our cause their own. I ask them to stand calm and firm and united in this time of trial. The task will be hard. There may be dark days ahead, and war can no longer be confined to the battlefield. But we can only do the right as we see the right, and reverently commit our cause to God.

If one and all we keep resolutely faithful to it, ready for whatever service or sacrifice it may demand, then, with God's help, we shall prevail.

May He bless and keep us all.

Note. From "With God's Help, We Shall Prevail," by King George VI, 1939, retrieved from http://www.americanrhetoric.com/speeches/kinggeorgevifirstradioaddress.htm. Reprinted from the public domain.

Name: _____ Date: _____

Theme/Concept

C3 — What message does he want to convey to the people of Britain about the war and Britain's involvement? Write the theme of his message as a tweet.

Inference

C2 — Does King George VI want to go to war? How do you know?

Textual Elements and Understanding

C1 — What reasons does King George VI provide for going to war?

WITH GOD'S HELP, WE SHALL PREVAIL

Name: _____   Date: _____

Comparison Ladder for "Propaganda Posters and World War II" and "With God's Help, We Shall Prevail"

This next ladder asks students to compare King George VI's speech with the U.S. WWII propaganda posters. As the country of origin is different for each selection, students are asked to examine the similarities and differences of the messages during the same time period.

Name: _____ Date: _____

Generalizations

B3 — If Britain were to have made a poster of King George's early war speech, what would it look like, based on his message? What would the caption be? Sketch it, using the same pattern as the U.S. WWII posters, and be ready to explain your sketch, using evidence from the articles.

Classifications

B2 — Based on the categories the OWI designated for WWII posters in the article, how would you categorize King George's speech? Why? What is King George asking of his people? Others?

Details

B1 — How does King George's message to Britain at the onset of WWII compare with the messages in the WWII posters from the United States after the war started? What are the common messages? Which ones are different?

COMPARISON LADDER FOR "PROPAGANDA POSTERS AND WORLD WAR II" AND "WITH GOD'S HELP, WE SHALL PREVAIL"

87

Above and Beyond: Doris "Dorie" Miller and Pearl Harbor

"Above and beyond the call of duty—Dorie Miller received the Navy Cross at Pearl Harbor, May 27, 1942" by David Stone Martin, 1943. Created for U.S. Office of War Information, Washington, DC: U.S. Government Printing Office. Reprinted from the public domain.

Prior to World War II, the Navy was segregated based on ethnicity. Under U.S. policies at the time, African Americans were not allowed to serve in combat roles. They served in the kitchen (known as the "mess") and carried out menial tasks on board the ship. African American naval soldiers did not receive any military or weaponry training. However, that did not stop them from defending their country. One mess attendant in particular, Doris "Dorie" Miller, became the first African American to be awarded the U.S. Navy Cross for his heroic actions during the bombing at Pearl Harbor, HI, on December 7, 1941.

While the *U.S.S. West Virginia* was docked in Pearl Harbor, Miller was working in the laundry facility below deck. This task was interrupted when men on the deck alerted the soldiers of the ongoing attack by the Japanese. Japanese planes began bombing the military base at Pearl Harbor and the naval ships docked there. All the men on the ship went to their assigned battle stations. Miller was ordered to carry the wounded seamen from the deck to a place of safety. After carrying the captain of the ship to safety, Miller took control of the .50 caliber anti-aircraft gun and although he did not have training, he began shooting at the Japanese fighter planes. Unfortunately, due to poor military records, there are numerous contradicting accounts about how many planes he shot down, with reports ranging from 0 to 5 planes. Miller manned the gun for about 15 minutes until he ran out of ammunition, and the ship needed to be evacuated because it was sinking.

After the battle, the press and the Navy referred to Miller as an unnamed "Negro mess attendant" who helped save others. However, a researcher, Lawrence Reddick, from the Schomburg Center for Research in Black Culture in Harlem learned his identity and shared it with African American newspapers. These newspapers worked with Civil Rights groups to lobby the government and Navy to ensure that Miller received an award for his actions during the battle. On May 27, 1942, Miller became the first African American to receive the U.S. Navy Cross and his image was featured on Navy posters.

References

Chester, R. K. (2013). "Negroes' number one hero": Doris Miller, Pearl Harbor, and retroactive multiculturalism in World War II remembrance. *American Quarterly, 65,* 31–61.

Hull, M. D. (2016). A Black hero's courage under fire. In M. D. Hull, *Naval history* (Vol. 30, pp. 56–62). Annapolis, MD: U.S. Naval Institute.

Joyner, M. R. (2015, April 10). Rethinking the Recognition of Doris Miller. *New Pittsburgh Courier.* Retrieved from http://newpittsburghcourier online.com/2015/04/10/rethinking-the-recognition-of-doris-miller/

Mueller, W. R. (1945). The Negro in the Navy. *Social Forces, 24,* 110–115.

Reddick, L. (1947). The Negro in the United States Navy during World War II. *The Journal of Negro History, 32,* 201–219.

Suid, L. (2001). Pearl Harbor: More or less. *Air Power History, 48*(3), 38–43.

Name: _____ Date: _____

Theme/Concept

C3 — Why did the poster caption say "Above and beyond the call of duty"? Create another poster and caption that explain the theme of Dorie Miller's story and teaches others about this event.

Inference

C2 — What inferences can you make about the type of man Dorie Miller was, based on this account you just read?

Textual Elements and Understanding

C1 — What events led to Dorie Miller's being recognized with the U.S. Navy Cross for his heroic acts? Name what these events were in a list. Why was this recognition significant?

ABOVE AND BEYOND: DORIS "DORIE" MILLER AND PEARL HARBOR

A New Kind of Snow Day for Students

by Erin Grisham

In the midst of the icy weather that's sweeping across the U.S. and closing down countless schools, many teachers must improvise their lesson plans and make sure students remain caught up. But with the increased availability of online resources, fors don't have to get in the way of students who need to learn material by the day of their final exams, or cause teachers to scramble.

An *Education Week* article, "Snow Days Turn Into E-Learning Days for Some Schools" by Alyssa Morones, describes how a new Ohio law will give state school districts the option to use up to three "e-learning days" instead of having snow days. The missed days wouldn't be made up during the summer holidays because students could do their work from home.

Ohio Superintendent Shelly Vaughn thinks e-learning days are a great compromise on bad weather days. "It's much better to have a day of e-learning instruction right now than if we held a makeup day when the weather's nice," Vaughn said. "It's hard to keep kids focused at that time of year."

Universities—admittedly much better at providing online resources than grade schools—have had excellent outlets for instructors to post reading assignments, quizzes, video lessons, etc. (Blackboard and Canvas come to mind). During bad weather days at the university level, web-based classes don't falter off course in the slightest. All the new resources available to schools can give teachers a way to make lessons more creative and interactive in ways that couldn't be done before. Mixing up the daily in-class routines with cyber lessons could keep students more engaged and allow them to become even more comfortable with technology.

Note. From "A new kind of snow day for students" by E. Grisham, 2014, published on the Prufrock Press blog, retrieved from http://blog.prufrock.com/blog/2014/2/5/a-new-kind-of-snow-day?rq=a%20new%20kind%20of%20snow%20day. Copyright 2014 Taylor & Francis. Reprinted with permission.

Name: _____ Date: _____

Consequences and Implications

A3

What might be some of the positive and negative implications for schools that decide to mandate e-learning during snow days? Create a T-chart to compare positive and negative implications, using information from the article and your own ideas.

Negative Implications	Positive Implications

Cause and Effect

A2

What are the effects of having "e-learning days" instead of snow days, according to the article?

Sequencing

A1

Sequence the reasons the author gives for having "a new kind of snow day."

A NEW KIND OF SNOW DAY FOR STUDENTS

Name: _____ Date: _____

Theme/Concept

C3

Write a response to the article, incorporating at least three different perspectives (i.e., students, teachers, parents, those who are poor, those who are wealthy). How would these groups feel about the change? List your thinking in the chart below.

Groups	Perspectives on E-Learning Snow Days
1.	
2.	
3.	

Inference

C2

What perspectives and arguments did the author not include? Can you think of groups and perspectives not represented? How does this exclusion of other perspectives impact the message?

Textual Elements and Understanding

C1

What is the author's perspective about "e-learning," based on the evidence provided? What reasons does she include in support of the idea?

Should Students Be Required to Wear School Uniforms?

Although traditionally adopted by private schools, more and more public schools are opting for mandatory uniform requirements. In 2008, only one eighth of public schools required students to wear uniforms. By 2011, that number had increased to one fifth. The trend toward adopting uniforms continues to rise, but not everyone agrees with the change. Supporters of uniforms say that they make schools safer while reducing economic disparity and honing student focus. Opponents say that uniforms threaten children's right to individuality and have no positive effects on behavior or academics.

Pros

Student safety is a significant factor when schools are considering a uniform code. One school in Long Beach, CA, studied assault, fighting, robbery, and vandalism rates before and after it adopted uniforms in 1994. The school found that after 2 years of adopting uniforms, these crime rates dropped significantly. There were fewer firearm and drug-related incidents as well. Uniforms can also make it easier to keep track of students and spot intruders in a school. Studies have also found that teachers perceive their students more positively when they wear uniforms; teachers assume students are better behaved and more academically proficient when they wear uniforms. Discipline, safety, and dress seem to be linked in the minds of educators in many schools.

Other studies found that adopting uniforms improved attendance, graduation rates, and discipline. A 2010 study found that uniforms helped to decrease the absence rates of girls in middle and high school. Another study saw girls' language test scores improve by three percentage points after uniforms were required. School leaders have found that mandatory uniforms make it easier for students to prepare for school in the morning—meaning fewer late arrivals. Uniforms also allow teachers to spend less time disciplining students for dress code infractions. This added learning time then benefits students who spend more time in class.

School leaders also note that the removal of fashion concerns allows students to focus more on their schoolwork. They spend less time worrying about outfits and fitting in because everyone wears the same clothes. Uniforms can help to make differences in students' economic statuses less visible; privileged students, for example, will be wearing the same outfits as their less privileged classmates. Income distinctions can become less obvious, allowing for decreased peer pressure and bullying. In fact, 86% of school leaders said that uniforms had positive effects on peer pressure, while 64% noted that uniforms reduced bullying.

Most parents and teachers support mandatory uniforms, according to multiple surveys. Uniforms can actually save parents money—families can spend less on school outfits because there are fewer choices. The estimated cost per child is $150 or less per year.

Finally, supporters contend that uniforms do not infringe on the students' right to free expression. Students can still express their individuality in other ways. A 2012 survey found that 58% of eighth graders felt that they could still express themselves, even when wearing uniforms. In this way, mandatory clothing does not discriminate or deny free speech.

Cons

The main argument against mandatory uniforms involves the students' right to express themselves. Critics argue that uniforms can restrict the freedom of students as guaranteed by the First Amendment. Choice in clothing can be critical to the developing identities of kids and teens. There are also cases in which certain clothes can be part of supporting social awareness. At one school, students were sent home for wearing pink T-shirts in support of breast cancer awareness. This kind of rigid interpretation of rules discourages creativity and social participation.

Uniforms can also actually increase violence and lower achievement. A 2007 study found that implementing the use of uniforms actually increased violence and discipline incidents in already violent schools. The study found no positive effect on behavior, and even suggested that the introduction of uniforms might have contributed to negative effects in the school. Uniform mandates have also been accused of taking attention away from other efforts to improve safety in schools and to boost student performance.

Opponents point out that uniforms can actually emphasize the economic divisions they attempt to erase. The majority of schools with mandatory uniforms are located in poorer neighborhoods, meaning that uniforms are becoming associated with poverty and, troublingly, with minorities. Schools with a minority population of 50% or more were 24 times more likely to require uniforms than schools with a minority population of

5–19%. Uniforms also cannot conceal social status. Poorer families may not have the money to replace damaged uniforms, meaning children will come to school in torn or tattered clothing. This wear on the uniforms will be more obvious when compared to the state of the uniforms of more privileged children.

This kind of comparing of the self to others (i.e., social comparison) is a large concern for many students. When everyone is wearing the same clothing, it is much easier to see small differences between students. This comparing can lead to poor self-image, especially in girls whose body differences (tall, short, plus size) become obvious when every girl wears the same skirt or top. A 2003 study from Arizona State University found that in nonuniform schools, students had better self-concept.

Students themselves largely oppose uniforms. One survey conducted in 2012 found that 90% of students did not like school uniforms. Most students did not believe uniforms made them safer or connected them more to their classmates. Instead, students believed they should be free to choose their own clothes and save their families money. After all, the uniform industry takes in $1 billion each year from school uniform purchases. It is possible that uniforms might be commercially, not academically, driven. These concerns make many students and families mistrustful of adopting school uniforms.

In summary, there are positive and negative components to adopting school uniforms. Which side are you on?

References

ProCon.org. (n.d.). *Should students have to wear school uniforms?* Retrieved from http://school-uniforms.procon.org

Public School Review. (n.d.). *Public school uniforms: The pros and cons for your child.* Retrieved from http://www.publicschoolreview.com/blog/public-school-uniforms-the-pros-and-cons-for-your-child

Name: _____ Date: _____

Consequences and Implications

A3

What are the potential positive and negative consequences of schools' adopting a school uniform policy?

Cause and Effect

A2

What are the effects of schools' requiring school uniforms on various groups? What are the effects on businesses, students, parents, teachers, and other groups? Use the article to support your answer. Make a chart to show each stakeholder group and the impact of mandatory school uniforms for each group.

Sequencing

A1

What arguments are most important to each side? List the top three arguments on school uniforms that are most convincing to you, from most to least. Provide a rationale for their importance.

SHOULD STUDENTS BE REQUIRED TO WEAR SCHOOL UNIFORMS?

Name: _____ Date: _____

Creative Synthesis

D3

What arguments were not included in the article that may be important? Write an opinion essay, either pro or con, that incorporates information from the article as well as your own arguments and discredits the opposite side. Write a conclusion to your essay.

Summarizing

D2

Summarize the purpose of considering school uniforms as an option, based on the arguments given for each side.

Paraphrasing

D1

In your own words, what are the pro and con arguments for school uniform policies?

SHOULD STUDENTS BE REQUIRED TO WEAR SCHOOL UNIFORMS?

Part III: Readings and Student Ladder Sets for Fiction and Nonfiction Comparisons

Part III includes the selected readings and accompanying question sets for each nonfiction and fiction comparison selection. Each reading is followed by one or two sets of questions; each set is aligned to one of the six ladder skills.

The ladder skills covered by each selection are as follows:

Reading Titles	Ladders	Comparison Ladder
The Decision to Go to the Moon	C	C
But Outer Space	C, F	
Afternoon on a Hill	C	B
Solvay Process Company Photograph	B, D	
Good Books	C, F	D
Bringing Literature to the Streets	A	
The Vain Jackdaw	C	C
Sandra Cisneros	C, E	

The Decision to Go to the Moon
John F. Kennedy, May 25, 1961

. . . If this capsule history of our progress teaches us anything, it is that man, in his quest for knowledge and progress, is determined and cannot be deterred. The exploration of space will go ahead, whether we join in it or not, and it is one of the great adventures of all time, and no nation which expects to be the leader of other nations can expect to stay behind in the race for space.

Those who came before us made certain that this country rode the first waves of the industrial revolutions, the first waves of modern invention, and the first wave of nuclear power, and this generation does not intend to founder in the backwash of the coming age of space. We mean to be a part of it—we mean to lead it. For the eyes of the world now look into space, to the moon and to the planets beyond, and we have vowed that we shall not see it governed by a hostile flag of conquest, but by a banner of freedom and peace. We have vowed that we shall not see space filled with weapons of mass destruction, but with instruments of knowledge and understanding.

Yet the vows of this Nation can only be fulfilled if we in this Nation are first, and, therefore, we intend to be first. In short, our leadership in science and in industry, our hopes for peace and security, our obligations to ourselves as well as others, all require us to make this effort, to solve these mysteries, to solve them for the good of all men, and to become the world's leading space-faring nation.

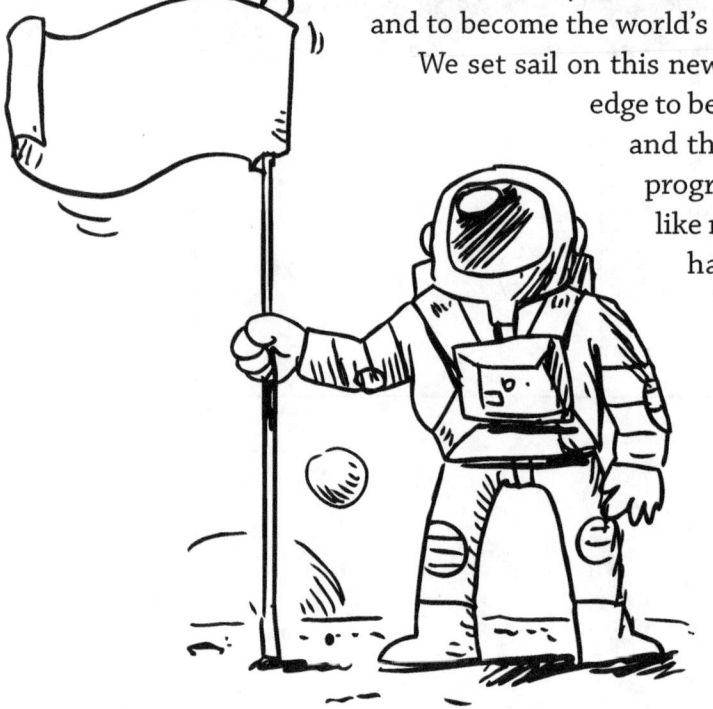

We set sail on this new sea because there is new knowledge to be gained, and new rights to be won, and they must be won and used for the progress of all people. For space science, like nuclear science and all technology, has no conscience of its own. Whether it will become a force for good or ill depends on man, and only if the United States occupies a position of pre-eminence can we help decide whether this new ocean will be a sea of peace or a new terrifying theater of war. I do not say that we should or will go unprotected against the hostile misuse of space any more than we go unprotected against the hostile use of land or sea, but I do say that space can be explored and mastered without feeding the fires of war, without repeating the mistakes that man has made in extending his writ around this globe of ours.

There is no strife, no prejudice, no national conflict in outer space as yet. Its hazards are hostile to us all. Its conquest deserves the best of all mankind, and its opportunity for peaceful cooperation may never come again. But why, some say, the moon? Why choose this as our goal? And they may well ask why climb the highest mountain? Why, 35 years ago, fly the Atlantic? . . .

We choose to go to the moon. We choose to go to the moon in this decade and do the other things, not because they are easy, but because they are hard, because that goal will serve to organize and measure the best of our energies and skills, because that challenge is one that we are willing to accept, one we are unwilling to postpone, and one which we intend to win, and the others, too.

It is for these reasons that I regard the decision last year to shift our efforts in space from low to high gear as among the most important decisions that will be made during my incumbency in the office of the Presidency.

Note. From "The Decision to Go to the Moon," by J. F. Kennedy, May 25, 1961, speech before a Joint Session of Congress. Retrieved from http://history.nasa.gov/moondec.html. Reprinted from the public domain.

Name: _____ Date: _____

Theme/Concept

C3

What is the main theme of President Kennedy's speech? How do you know? Create a graphic organizer to illustrate the theme and the evidence to support it from the speech.

Inference

C2

Why was it important for the United States to lead the effort to go to the moon, according to President Kennedy? Summarize his perspective from the speech.

Textual Elements and Understanding

C1

What sequence of events led to President Kennedy's supporting the United States going to the moon? Paraphrase them in your own words.

THE DECISION TO GO TO THE MOON

Name: _____   Date: _____

But Outer Space
by Robert Frost

But outer Space,
At least this far,
For all the fuss
Of the populace
Stays more popular
Than populous.

Note. From "But Outer Space" in *In the Clearing* by R. Frost, 1962, New York, NY: Henry Holt. Copyright 1962 by Henry Holt. Reprinted with permission.

Name: _____ Date: _____

Theme/Concept

C3

What does Frost think about exploration in outer space, based on the poem? Does he agree or disagree? How do you know?

Inference

C2

Why do you think Frost started the poem with the word "but"? How does that affect the meaning of the poem?

Textual Elements and Understanding

C1

Highlight some of the important words in the poem that help us understand it. Why are these words important?

BUT OUTER SPACE

Name: _____ Date: _____

Playing With Words

F3

What impact does the use of three similar but different words (i.e., populace, populous, popular) have on the reader? How does it affect you?

Thinking About Words

F2

Rewrite the poem by substituting a word or phrase for each of the words in F1.

Understanding Words

F1

What do the words *populace*, *popular*, and *populous* mean? What are the similarities and differences of each word?

BUT OUTER SPACE

Comparison Ladder for "The Decision to Go to the Moon" and "But Outer Space"

Students are asked to compare an excerpt from JFK's speech defending America's quest for a moon landing with a poem, entitled "But Outer Space" by Robert Frost. Frost's poem was published about a year after Kennedy's speech.

Name: _____ Date: _____

COMPARISON LADDER FOR "THE DECISION TO GO TO THE MOON" AND "BUT OUTER SPACE"

Theme/Concept

C3

How does each author's idea of exploration differ? Pretend you are either President Kennedy or Robert Frost. Write a letter to the other that supports your point of view about exploration in space and provides evidence from "your" perspective.

Inference

C2

What is the purpose of the poem? Of the speech? How are they similar yet different?

Textual Elements and Understanding

C1

Create a Venn diagram to compare what President Kennedy says and what Frost says about outer space.

Afternoon on a Hill

by Edna St. Vincent Millay

I will be the gladdest thing
Under the sun!
I will touch a hundred flowers
And not pick one.

I will look at cliffs and clouds
With quiet eyes,
Watch the wind bow down the grass,
And the grass rise.

And when lights begin to show
Up from the town,
I will mark which must be mine,
And then start down!

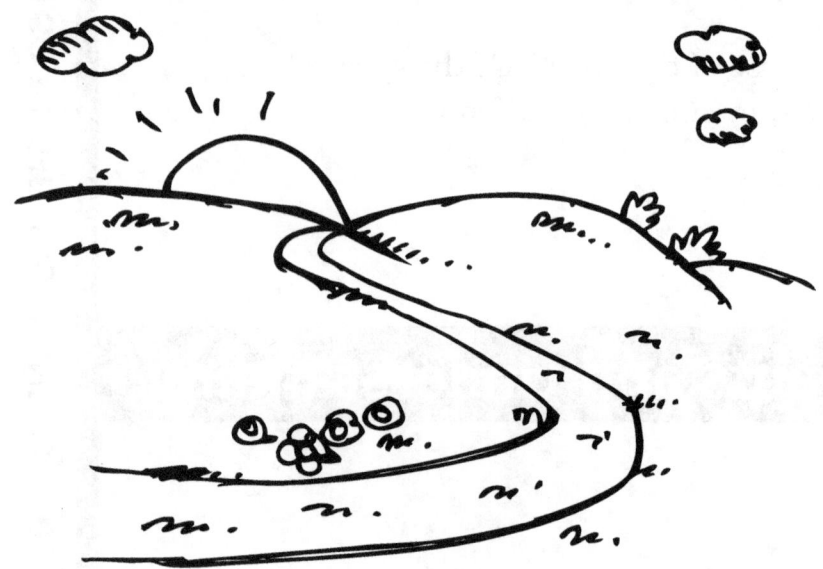

Name: _____ Date: _____

Theme/Concept

C3

If you could create a symbol for this poem, what would it be? Why?

Inference

C2

How does the author feel about nature? How do you know?

Textual Elements and Understanding

C1

Draw a picture of the setting of this poem and be ready to explain your thinking, using evidence from the poem.

Solvay Process Company Photograph

The Solvay Process Company, founded in 1881 in Syracuse, NY, manufactured soda ash using a patented process known as the Solvay process—named after the last name of two brothers from Belgium who perfected the process. *Note*. From Solvay Process Co.'s works, Syracuse, c. 1890–1901, Library of Congress Prints and Photographs Division, Washington, DC, retrieved from http://www.loc.gov/pictures/item/det1994007647/PP. Reprinted from the public domain.

Name: _____ Date: _____

Generalizations

B3

What might you infer from the photograph about the development of factories during the Industrial Revolution? Write a true statement or generalization about the Industrial Revolution's impact that is supported by the photographic details.

Classifications

B2

Based on the photograph's details, what do you think were the effects of industrialization on the following: America's economy? Living conditions? Nature? Make a chart to organize your ideas.

Details

B1

What details do you notice in the photograph? Make a list.

SOLVAY PROCESS COMPANY PHOTOGRAPH

Name: _____ Date: _____

Creative Synthesis

D3

Find at least three additional paintings or photos that depict the Industrial Revolution in the United States or internationally. What do these images have in common with the photograph? With each other? This website will get you started in your search: http://www.history.com/topics/industrial-revolution/pictures

Summarizing

D2

In your own words, explain why this photograph is important in our understanding of the Industrial Revolution. Do you think it is an accurate depiction of other American places? Why or why not?

Paraphrasing

D1

Why do you think the photographer framed the photograph as he did? What significance does that have on the interpretation?

SOLVAY PROCESS COMPANY PHOTOGRAPH

112

Name: _____ Date: _____

Comparison Ladder for "Afternoon on a Hill" and "Solvay Process Company Photograph"

During the Industrial Revolution, many people in the United States and abroad were conflicted about the impact of industrial progress on nature. Students are asked to compare a photograph taken during the Industrial Revolution with a poem about the love of nature.

Name: _____ Date: _____

COMPARISON LADDER FOR "AFTERNOON ON A HILL" AND "SOLVAY PROCESS COMPANY PHOTOGRAPH"

Generalizations

B3

What have been the consequences of industry and development on the natural environment? Write an argument that examines the pros and cons of allowing industrial development to proceed, regardless of its impact on natural settings.

Classifications

B2

How would you describe the cause and effect relationship of industrialization and nature, based on the poem and the photograph?

Details

B1

Make a list of details about nature shown in the photograph and in the poem by completing the following chart:

	Details	What Is Implied About Nature
Photograph		
Poem		

114

Good Books
by Edgar Guest

Good books are friendly things to own.
If you are busy they will wait.
They will not call you on the phone
Or wake you if the hour is late.

They stand together row by row,
Upon the low shelf or the high.
But if you're lonesome this you know:
You have a friend or two nearby.

The fellowship of books is real.
They're never noisy when you're still.
They won't disturb you at your meal.
They'll comfort you when you are ill.

The lonesome hours they'll always share.
When slighted they will not complain.
And though for them you've ceased to care
Your constant friends they'll still remain.

Good books your faults will never see
Or tell about them round the town.
If you would have their company
You merely have to take them down.

They'll help you pass the time away,
They'll counsel give if that you need.
He has true friends for night and day
Who has a few good books to read.

Name: _____ Date: _____

Theme/Concept

C3

What is the main purpose of a book, according to the poet? In a poem, create your own list about the value of a good book, modelled after Guest's poem.

Inference

C2

What does the author mean by "When slighted they will not complain"? Explain in a short paragraph.

Textual Elements and Understanding

C1

What are the benefits of having a few good books to own, according to the poet? List them.

GOOD BOOKS

Name: _____ Date: _____

Playing With Words

F3

Write your own poem of two stanzas about something that you enjoy that follows the same rhyming pattern as the Guest poem and uses the literary device of personification as seen in the poem. (It may be helpful to brainstorm how the topic you chose to write about is like a person before writing.)

Thinking About Words

F2

Personification is the application of human attributes to nonhuman things. How does the author use personification in this poem? Complete the following sentence using evidence from the poem: A book is like a person because . . .

Understanding Words

F1

Listen to the poem read aloud. What images come to mind? Sketch one picture that comes to your mind when you read this poem. Compare your drawing to those of your classmates.

Bringing Literature to the Streets

The closing of bookstores and libraries across the globe has changed the way people read literature. With the rise of the eBook and Amazon, fewer people are engaging with physical books and bookstores. To encourage reading in communities, companies are working to advertise literature like never before: on the streets, in buses, on coffee cups, and even in vending machines!

One such company, Coffee House Press, printed excerpts of poetry and prose by diverse Minneapolis writers on 10,000 coffee sleeves. According to managing director Caroline Casey, "It's a way of putting literature in a public space and giving people a literary experience that isn't reading a book." The company wants to encourage people to see literature as accessible and enjoyable, not as a pastime reserved for the elite. Coffee Sleeves Conversation brings literature to consumers' daily lives while also sparking discussion about current issues of the day.

A similar project in France brings literature straight to the vending machine. Short Edition allows pedestrians to choose from 600 free short stories of varying lengths. These stories are then dispensed from the machine and can be read on lunch breaks or during work commutes. The idea of reading during travel also inspired Poems on the Underground, a project that places poetry on the walls of Tube trains in London. Founder Judith Chernaik explained the appeal of this project: "The tube poems are popular because they offer an escape from the combined pressures of advertising and daily work. They invite the traveller to share the dreams and visions of another human being, speaking across time and place."

Others are doing their part to take literature to the streets by delivering physical copies of books to those without access. In Argentina, Raul Lemesoff created a vehicle with shelves that can hold up to 900 books. For World Book Day in 2015, Lemesoff delivered free books to citizens across Argentina using this "weapon of mass instruction." Such vehicles can be found in other areas as well. Illinois' Bloomington Public Library created a "bookmobile" that can travel around the area, offering access to books, magazines, DVDs, and video games. This vehicle is a useful addition to the

Bloomington community, which recently suffered from the closing of a local bookstore.

These individuals and companies were inspired by the concept of guerrilla marketing, an unconventional marketing approach that brings advertising to unexpected places. Guerrilla marketing relies on consumers' imaginations and is not supported by a large budget. Though unusual, the tactic seems to be working. According to Thales Teixeira, a Harvard Business School marketing professor, "Letters and words have symbolic value to people. We still as a society have some fascination with books."

Even kids and young adults can get involved by sharing literature with their communities. The Little Free Library program allows people to construct and install small libraries in public spaces. People can then borrow and lend books to the greater community. For example, Patrick Hester, a Boy Scout in northern Indianapolis, recently built four Little Free Libraries for his Eagle Scout Project. Although the process of raising funds, figuring out locations, and building the libraries was challenging, Hester succeeded in building new opportunities for reading in his neighborhood.

As our world continues to modernize, these tactics may change and evolve. But whatever new marketing strategies arise, one thing is clear: people will always look for new ways to share and read literature.

References

Little Free Library. (2016). *Library build case study: Eagle Scout project.* Retrieved from http://littlefreelibrary.org/eagle-scout-library-build

Petrovich, H. (2015). Bookmobile brings literature to the streets. *Vidette Online.* http://www.videtteonline.com/viewpoint/bookmobile-brings-literature-to-the-streets/article_01e8cbf7-6522-55b2-bd95-a03628930f58.html

Schwab, K. (2016). Taking literature to the streets. *The Atlantic.* Retrieved from http://www.theatlantic.com/entertainment/archive/2016/01/taking-literature-to-the-streets/432558

Name: _____ Date: _____

Consequences and Implications

A3

The article cites many positive reasons to bring literature to the streets. Are there any negatives? Provide possible negative consequences or different perspectives that the author may not have thought about or that may disagree with this article's purpose. In an essay, create an argument against the use of guerilla tactics, taking into account the article's perspective.

Cause and Effect

A2

What are the known effects of the various projects on literacy and reading engagement? Create a T-chart. In column 1, list each project mentioned in the article and in column 2, cite the effects of the project. What long-term effects might the projects have?

Project	Effects of the Project

Sequencing

A1

What events led to several projects focused on "bringing literature to the streets"?

Name: _____ Date: _____

Comparison Ladder for "Good Books" and "Bringing Literature to the Streets"

Asking students to compare two forms of writing, both on the same topic, allows them to see how words and images can be used so differently in the formation of meaning. Students will now compare the nonfiction writing on the use of literature in common everyday places with the poem on the value of a good book.

Name: _____ Date: _____

COMPARISON LADDER FOR "GOOD BOOKS" AND "BRINGING LITERATURE TO THE STREETS"

D3 — Creative Synthesis

Survey others in your class and your family (at least 20 people) about whether or not they prefer to have physical books or electronic books to read. Also collect data on:
- each person's age,
- his or her purpose for reading,
- type of readings (i.e., magazine, newspaper, novels, nonfiction, and/or poetry),
- and the frequency with which he or she reads (i.e., hourly, twice a day, daily, every other day, weekly).

Create a graph of your findings and describe the answers to the questions posed about your results by interpreting your graph for an audience.
- What patterns do you notice?
- Does the age of an individual matter with respect to the type of reading material preferred?
- Does the purpose of reading relate to frequency?
- How do your findings relate to the poem and article messages?

D2 — Summarizing

Summarize the common messages of both readings by writing 2–3 true statements that apply to each.

Paraphrasing

D1

What details from the poem and article suggest that access to books and literature is important?

The Vain Jackdaw
by Aesop

One day the king said that he wanted to appoint a ruler over the birds, and named a day on which they were to appear before his throne, when he would select the most beautiful of them all to be their ruler. In order to look their best, the birds went to the banks of a stream, where they busied themselves in washing and preening their feathers. The Jackdaw was there along with the rest, and realized that, with his ugly plumage, he would have no chance of being chosen as he was. He waited till they were all gone, and then picked up the most fancy and outlandish feathers they had dropped, and fastened them to himself so that he looked better than any of them. When the appointed day came, the birds assembled before the king's throne and the king was most impressed with the Jackdaw. He was about to make the Jackdaw the ruler, when the rest of the birds attacked the ruler-elect, tore off his borrowed feathers, and exposed him for the Jackdaw that he was.

Name: _____ Date: _____

Theme/Concept

C3

What is the moral of this fable? Retitle the fable and then make it a bumper sticker or tweet.

Inference

C2

Why did the other birds attack the Jackdaw? What was the result?

Textual Elements and Understanding

C1

Based on the evidence from the fable, sketch a scene from the story and provide captions that show how your scene matches the information provided.

THE VAIN JACKDAW

Sandra Cisneros

Sandra Cisneros is a popular Latina American novelist whose book, *The House on Mango Street,* has sold more than two million copies. Her work explores the cultural struggles that many Mexican-American women face.

Sandra was born in Chicago in 1954 to a Mexican father and a Chicano mother. Her family moved frequently when she was a child and took multiple trips to Mexico to visit her father's relatives. Although Chicago was the site of much of her childhood, she never felt connected to the city, an idea she would explore later in her books. Throughout her childhood, Sandra's mother encouraged her to read and break some of the traditionally known female roles expected of her. Sandra found reading a nice way to escape. She began writing poetry in high school and eventually became the editor of her school's literary magazine.

After high school, she pursued her bachelor's degree at Chicago Loyola University. She then went on to receive her Master of Fine Arts in creative writing at the University of Iowa. Sandra's time at Iowa helped her to develop her writing voice and cement her goals. Most of her classmates came from more privileged backgrounds, and she found that she wrote about different topics and in a different style than many of her colleagues. However, she decided to embrace her unique viewpoint and began writing a novel.

After graduating from Iowa in 1978, she worked in various positions—as a teacher, a college recruiter, and a counselor for minority students. She returned to Chicago, and then lived in several other places, including France and Greece, where she had received fellowships to work on her novel. In 1984, she finally published *The House on Mango Street*, a novel about growing up in Chicago, to critical acclaim. Readers enjoyed the authenticity of the characters and the simplicity of Sandra's style.

The House on Mango Street, along with her later short stories and poetry collections, revolved around the themes of alienation and cultural displacement. Sandra drew much of her inspiration from her own childhood, but insists that the book is not merely autobiographical. The characters face the pressures of living in an uncomfortable city while trying to navigate the cultural traditions still expected of them by their families. Sandra detailed

the power struggles that many immigrant families and second-generation children face. How does a person learn to live with independence and self-respect while still honoring her cultural traditions?

In the late 1980s, Sandra divided her time between California and Texas, publishing poetry and a collection of short stories. These other works expanded on the themes she had developed in her novel. Sandra grew comfortable with her writing voice and her identity—as a working-class, independent Mexican-American woman. Her writing reflects this assurance of identity, and *The House on Mango Street* has become required reading at many schools. Sandra has also published a bilingual picture book, *Hairs/Pelitos*, for young readers ages 5–8.

Cisneros has received many accolades for her work. She has won the American Book Award, the Lannan Foundation Literary Award, and the Texas Medal of the Arts, as well as various fellowships throughout her career. Readers continue to enjoy the directness and poignancy of her writing.

References

Biography.com. (n.d.). *Sandra Cisneros*. Retrieved from http://www.biography.com/people/sandra-cisneros-185853

CliffsNotes. (n.d.). *Critical essays: Form and language as characterization in Cisneros' fiction*. Retrieved from http://www.cliffsnotes.com/literature/h/the-house-on-mango-street-woman-hollering-creek-other-stories/critical-essays/form-and-language-as-characterization-in-cisneros-fiction

CliffsNotes. (n.d.). *Sandra Cisneros biography*. Retrieved from http://www.cliffsnotes.com/literature/h/the-house-on-mango-street-woman-hollering-creek-other-stories/sandra-cisneros-biography

GradeSaver. (n.d.). *Biography of Sandra Cisneros*. Retrieved from http://www.gradesaver.com/author/sandra-cisneros

Juffer, J. (n.d.). *Sandra Cisneros: Biographical note*. Retrieved from http://www.english.illinois.edu/maps/poets/a_f/cisneros/bio.htm

Name: _____ Date: _____

Theme/Concept

C3

If you could identify one theme of Cisneros's life, what would it be and why? Use examples from her life to justify your response.

Inference

C2

What effect did Cisneros's life experiences have on her writing and later success?

Textual Elements and Understanding

C1

Create a timeline of the most important events of Cisneros's life. Instead of using specific dates, use the categories of childhood, college, and adulthood to sequence important life events.

SANDRA CISNEROS

Name: _____ Date: _____

Using Emotion

E3

What is the difference between celebrating uniqueness and feeling different? How did this apply to Cisneros's life? Can you recall a time when you felt different and did not want to celebrate it? Describe the event in a picture or poem.

Expressing Emotion

E2

How did Sandra Cisneros's unique perspective and experiences impact her writing? What perspectives or experiences in your life make you unique? How are your perspectives similar to or different from Cisneros's?

Understanding Emotion

E1

What were Sandra Cisneros's struggles growing up as a child of first-generation Mexican Americans? List what they were, based on the biography.

SANDRA CISNEROS

Name: _____ Date: _____

Comparison Ladder for "The Vain Jackdaw" and "Sandra Cisneros"

In the following ladder, students are asked to examine how the theme of individuality and conformity is evident in the fable, "The Vain Jackdaw," and in Sandra Cisneros's life.

Name: _____ Date: _____

COMPARISON LADDER FOR "THE VAIN JACKDAW" AND "SANDRA CISNEROS"

Theme/Concept

C3

How does the theme of individuality versus conformity play out in Cisneros's life and in the fable? Create a Venn diagram to show the relationship between the two readings, based on the theme.

Inference

C2

What would have happened, do you think, if Cisneros had tried to ignore her past to write the same way as everyone else? Why? Compare her situation to that of the Jackdaw in the fable.

Textual Elements and Understanding

C1

Describe the character traits of Cisneros in the table below. How was each trait helpful in developing her capacity to write for publication and ultimately public acclaim? Record in the table.

Character Trait	How It Was Helpful

Appendix A

Pre- and Postassessments With Scoring Rubric

Preassessment

The Deepest Hole Ever Dug

Could humans travel to the center of the Earth? If you looked at the deepest hole ever dug, you'd probably answer no.

The Kola Superdeep Borehole, located on the Kola Peninsula of Russia, started off as part of a subterranean version of the Space Race. In 1970, Russian scientists worked to dig as deeply as possible into the center of the Earth, hoping to exceed findings from U.S.-led Project Mohole, off the coast of Mexico, which ran out of funding in 1966. Until that time, geologists could only theorize about what lay in the Earth's crust.

The Russian project continued until 1994, when the scientists reached temperatures too prohibitively high for their drills—a mega-burning 356° F! At that point, the hole reached down 7.5 miles—farther than the deepest point of the ocean (6.8 miles), but still quite a way from the Earth's inner core (roughly 3,950 to 4,000 miles from the surface). The scientists never even made it past the Earth's first layer (the crust, which lies about 22 miles deep).

Along the way, the scientists made some fascinating discoveries, including free water deeper than ever believed to exist and old fossils from single-celled organisms, both found about 4 miles below the surface. This discovery was most intriguing because these "microfossils" were found within intact organic compounds, something surprising given the extreme pressures and temperatures of the surrounding rock.

According to Smithsonian.com, scientists are now hoping to go even deeper into the Earth, with international scientists planning a dig to the Earth's mantle. Before they can get there, however, they have to overcome monumental engineering roadblocks (including those blistering temperatures!) and the hefty billion-dollar price tag for such a project. Do you think they'll make it?

References

Ask Smithsonian. (2015). What's the deepest we've ever dug into the Earth? *Smithsonian Teen Tribune*. Retrieved from http://tweentribune.com/article/teen/whats-deepest-weve-ever-dug-earth

Hamilton, K. (2015). What's at the bottom of the deepest hole on Earth? *IFL Science*. Retrieved from http://www.iflscience.com/environment/deepest-hole-world

Morton, E. (2014). Beneath this metal cap is the world's deepest hole. *Slate.* Retrieved from http://www.slate.com/blogs/atlas_obscura/2014/05/08/kola_superdeep_borehole_is_the_world_s_deepest_hole.html

Name: _____   Date: _____

Preassessment: Questions

Read and answer each question, using evidence from the reading to support your ideas.

1. What are the implications of digging a hole deep into the Earth's crust? Explain, using evidence from the article.

   _____
   _____
   _____
   _____
   _____
   _____
   _____

2. What do the first two sentences say about humans not traveling to the center of the Earth? Use evidence from the remainder of the article to support your answer.

   _____
   _____
   _____
   _____
   _____
   _____
   _____

Name: _____ Date: _____

3. Write two generalizations about the Earth's inner core. Explain why these statements are true, using evidence from the article.

   _____
   _____
   _____
   _____
   _____
   _____
   _____

4. Create an original title for "The Deepest Hole Ever Dug" and justify in a short response why this title is a good one, based on what you have read.

   _____
   _____
   _____
   _____
   _____
   _____
   _____

Name: _____   Date: _____

Postassessment

Laptop vs. Longhand: The Benefits of Handwritten Notes

by Katy McDowall

There's little use denying technology's importance in the classroom. Students and teachers can collaborate with ease, and students can access a wealth of information with one click. All the same, laptops and tablets in the classroom have been the source of some debate, namely because of their propensity to cause distraction. Games, social media, and other activities can oftentimes be more popular than typing notes. And even when laptops are being used for note taking, a recent study in *Psychological Science* found that typing doesn't serve students as well as old-fashioned longhand.

Researchers performed three experiments in which college students watched 15-minute TED talks and either took notes by hand or on a laptop that was disconnected from the Internet (to avoid distractions). The participants were then tested on the lectures after 30 minutes—or, in one experiment, after a week and a short study session.

The results were the same: laptop users took more notes than those who wrote by hand. But students who wrote out their notes performed better because they paraphrased concepts into their own words, remembering more of the lecture. Students who used laptops were more likely to type out the lecture verbatim, "thus hurting learning." Even when participants in the second experiment were told not to type verbatim, it did nothing to "prevent this deleterious behavior."

The problem for laptop users? They may be able to take down notes faster than writing by hand, but they do not process as much information. Longhand note takers have to take more care in selecting what to include in their notes because it's harder to keep up with what's being said in a lecture than when typing. For both types of note takers, more notes can be beneficial, but not when "mindlessly transcribing content."

Note. From "Laptop vs. longhand: The benefits of handwritten notes" by K. McDowall, 2014, published on the Prufrock Press blog, retrieved from http://blog.prufrock.com/blog/2014/9/11/laptop-vs-longhand-the-benefits-of-handwritten-notes?rq=longhand. Copyright 2014 Taylor & Francis. Reprinted with permission.

Name: _____ Date: _____

Postassessment: Questions

Read and answer each question, using evidence from the reading to support your ideas.

1. What are the implications of both writing and using laptops on learning? Explain, using evidence from the article.

   _____
   _____
   _____
   _____
   _____
   _____
   _____

2. Should students write their answers or use a laptop, according to the article? Explain your answer, using the information provided.

   _____
   _____
   _____
   _____
   _____
   _____
   _____

Name: _____ Date: _____

3. Write two generalizations that support writing longhand instead of using a computer. Now write two generalizations that support using a computer. Support each statement, using evidence from the article.

   _____
   _____
   _____
   _____
   _____
   _____

4. Create an original title for "Laptop vs. Longhand" and justify in a short response why this title is a good one, based on what you have read.

   _____
   _____
   _____
   _____
   _____
   _____

Name: _____ Date: _____

Assessment Scoring Rubric

Question	Points				
	0	1	2	3	4
1 **Implications and Consequences (Ladder A)**	Provides no response or response is inappropriate to the task demand	Limited, vague, inaccurate; rewords the prompt or copies from the text	Response is somewhat accurate and makes sense but does not adequately address all components of the question or provide rationale from the text	Response is accurate; answers all parts of the question; provides a rationale that justifies the response but lacks interpretation or thorough evidence	Response is well written, specific, logical, interpretive; correctly answers all parts of the question, incorporates thorough evidence from the text
2 **Generalization (Ladder B)**	Provides no response or response is inappropriate to the task demand	Limited, vague, inaccurate; rewords the prompt or copies from text	Response is accurate but the generalizations are literal and limited	Generalizations are accurate and mostly synthesize the text but lack thorough justification or complete synthesis	Generalizations are interpretive with substantial justification or reasoning from the text
3 **Inference (Ladder C)**	Provides no response or response is inappropriate to the task demand	Limited, vague, inaccurate; rewords the prompt or copies from text	Accurate response but literal interpretation with no support from the text	Somewhat interpretive response but incomplete or with limited support from the text	Interpretive response with substantial support from the text
4 **Creative Synthesis (Ladder D)**	Provides no response or response is inappropriate to the task demand	Limited, vague, inaccurate; rewords the prompt or copies a phrase from text	Appropriate but literal title with little to no support	Interpretive title with limited reasoning or justification	Interpretive title that synthesizes the meaning of the piece, and uses extensive justification or reasoning from text

Appendix B

Record-Keeping Forms/Documents

This section includes a record-keeping sheet for each section. The forms can be used to keep track of student understanding and higher level thinking as they discuss different ladders or rungs. These may also be used in conjunction with the preassessments to diagnose and prescribe specific ladders based on student responses to each question by matching their response on each pretest question to a corresponding ladder and reading selection as part of differentiation.

Appendix B contains three record-keeping forms and documents:

- *Brainstorming/Answer Sheet*: This should be given to students for completion after reading a selection so that they may jot down ideas about the selection and questions prior to the discussion. The purpose of this sheet is to capture students' thoughts and ideas generated by reading the text. This sheet should act as a guide when students participate in group or class discussion.

- *My Reflection on Today's Reading and Discussion*: This form may be completed by the student after a group or class discussion on the readings. The reflection page is designed as a metacognitive approach to help students reflect on their strengths and weaknesses and to promote process skills. After discussion, students use the reflection page to record new ideas that were generated by others' comments and ideas.

- *Classroom Diagnostic Form*: These forms are for teachers and are designed to aid them in keeping track of the progress and skill mastery of their students. With these charts, teachers can look at student progress in relation to each ladder skill within a genre and select additional ladders and story selections based on student needs.

Name: _____ Date: _____

Brainstorming/Answer Sheet

Use this form to brainstorm thoughts and ideas about the readings and ladder questions before discussing with a partner.

143

Name: _____ Date: _____

My Reflection on Today's Reading and Discussion

Selection Title: _____

What I did well:

_____
_____
_____
_____

What I learned:

_____
_____
_____
_____

New ideas I have after discussion:

_____
_____
_____
_____

Next time I need to:

_____
_____
_____
_____

Classroom Diagnostic Form

Section 1: Science

Use this document to record student completion of ladder sets with the assessment of work.

0 = Needs Improvement   1 = Satisfactory   2 = Exceeds Expectations

Student Name	The Search for the Ninth Planet	The Aerodynamics of Crickets		Bumblebee Watch		A Pox on You!		In Tests of Mathematical Ability, Wolves Lead the Pack Over Dogs	Grace Murray Hopper, Computer Scientist	
	D	A	B (Comp. Ladder)	A	B (Comp. Ladder)	B	D	D	A	B

Classroom Diagnostic Form
Section 2: Math

Use this document to record student completion of ladder sets with the assessment of work.
0 = Needs Improvement   1 = Satisfactory   2 = Exceeds Expectations

Student Name	Making Math Fun		An Introduction to Magic Squares	Counting Like a Greek		Should Students Use Calculators During Math?	
	A	D	D	C	D	A	D

Classroom Diagnostic Form

Section 3: Social Studies

Use this document to record student completion of ladder sets with the assessment of work.

0 = Needs Improvement   1 = Satisfactory   2 = Exceeds Expectations

Student Name	Surrender Speech		The Fight for the Nez Perce Indian Territory		The Struggles of Young Factory Workers in the Industrial Revolution	Propaganda Posters and World War II			With God's Help, We Shall Prevail	
	C	D (Comp. Ladder)	A	D (Comp. Ladder)	A	B	C	B (Comp. Ladder)	C	B (Comp. Ladder)

Classroom Diagnostic Form, Section 3: Social Studies, *continued*

Student Name	Above and Beyond: Doris "Dorie" Miller and Pearl Harbor	A New Kind of Snow Day for Students		Should Students Be Required to Wear School Uniforms?	
	C	A	C	A	D

Classroom Diagnostic Form

Part III: Fiction and Nonfiction Comparisons

Use this document to record student completion of ladder sets with the assessment of work.

0 = Needs Improvement   1 = Satisfactory   2 = Exceeds Expectations

Student Name	The Decision to Go to the Moon		But Outer Space			Afternoon on a Hill			Solvay Process Company Photograph			Good Books		
	C	C (Comp. Ladder)	C	F	C (Comp. Ladder)	C	B (Comp. Ladder)		B	D	B (Comp. Ladder)	C	F	D (Comp. Ladder)

Classroom Diagnostic Form, Part III: Fiction and Nonfiction Comparisons, *continued*

Student Name	Bringing Literature to the Streets		The Vain Jackdaw		Sandra Cisneros		
	A	D (Comp. Ladder)	C	C (Comp. Ladder)	C	E	C (Comp. Ladder)

Appendix C

Alignment of the New Nonfiction Jacob's Ladder Program to the CCSS-ELA Standards

The alignment of the Jacob's Ladder nonfiction books to the Common Core State Standards (CCSS) may be best understood by examining the relevant sections of the ELA Nonfiction standards by grade level first, and seeing the corresponding ladders that require students to discuss and answer questions and do activities that address the standard under consideration.

Secondly, it is also important to review the textual choices selected, as many are advanced in reading level for the cited grade-level designation. For example, the following standards are cited as grade 3, yet many of the selected readings used are pitched two or more grade levels above, demonstrating the accelerated reading component of the program. Because many of the readings are accelerated, the processes, concepts and activities required are also accelerated and may meet partial or full standards in ELA above grade 3, too.

Thirdly, it is useful to consider each of the subject matter standards as well for coverage, as we have deliberately organized these books by subject area categories to diversify the readings and relate to the standards in each domain. For example, the use of the speeches of U.S. presidents meets the ELA standards for drawing inferences from text, determining main ideas, and explaining relationships between concepts, among others, in history. It also meets the social studies standards for analyzing events and individuals in history. The same issue may be true for science and math, especially as the standards call for the use of reasoning and the scientific process skill sets and interpreting authors' opinions/findings versus facts.

Finally, it is important to note that not all reading selections will have questions and activities that correspond to the ladders noted in the chart. We have indicated a correspondence if several selections have ladders that consistently make the connection to the standard cited. Other outcomes may be fulfilled for certain ladders, although not specifically listed. Moreover, merely having one match does not mean that a standard has been fully addressed. Teacher judgment needs to prevail in how much practice is needed in the type of higher order skills that these standards and ladders constitute, as well as which outcomes are best suited for a particular reading and ladder.

Alignment of New Nonfiction Jacob's Ladder Program to the CCSS-ELA Standards

	A	B	C	D	E	F
Reading: Key Ideas & Details						
CCSS.ELA-Literacy.RI.3.1 Ask and answer questions to demonstrate understanding of a text, referring explicitly to the text as the basis for the answers			X	X		
CCSS.ELA-Literacy.RI.3.2 Determine the main idea of a text; recount the key details and explain how they support the main idea.		X		X		
CCSS.ELA-Literacy.RI.3.3 Describe the relationship between a series of historical events, scientific ideas or concepts, or steps in technical procedures in a text, using language that pertains to time, sequence, and cause/effect.	X	X	X			
Reading: Craft & Structure						
CCSS.ELA-Literacy.RI.3.4 Determine the meaning of general academic and domain-specific words and phrases in a text relevant to a grade 3 topic or subject area.				X		
CCSS.ELA-Literacy.RI.3.6 Distinguish their own point of view from that of the author of a text.	X	X	X	X		
Reading: Integration of Knowledge & Ideas						
CCSS.ELA-Literacy.RI.3.7 Use information gained from illustrations (e.g., maps, photographs) and the words in a text to demonstrate understanding of the text (e.g., where, when, why, and how key events occur).	X			X		
CCSS.ELA-Literacy.RI.3.8 Describe the logical connection between particular sentences and paragraphs in a text (e.g., comparison, cause/effect, first/second/third in a sequence).	X	X	X			
CCSS.ELA-Literacy.RI.3.9 Compare and contrast the most important points and key details presented in two texts on the same topic.	X	X	X			

Alignment of New Nonfiction Jacob's Ladder Program to the CCSS-ELA Standards

	A	B	C	D	E	F
Reading: Range of Reading & Level of Text Complexity						
CCSS.ELA-Literacy.RI.3.10 By the end of the year, read and comprehend informational texts, including history/social studies, science, and technical texts, at the high end of the grades 2–3 text complexity band independently and proficiently.	X		X	X	X	X
Writing						
CCSS.ELA-Literacy.W.3.1 Write opinion pieces on topics or texts, supporting a point of view with reasons.	X		X	X		
CCSS.ELA-Literacy.W.3.2 Write informative/explanatory texts to examine a topic and convey ideas and information clearly.				X		
CCSS.ELA-Literacy.W.3.3 Write narratives to develop real or imagined experiences or events using effective technique, descriptive details, and clear event sequences.			X	X		
Writing: Production and Distribution of Writing						
*CCSS.ELA-Literacy.W.3.4 With guidance and support from adults, produce writing in which the development and organization are appropriate to task and purpose. (Grade-specific expectations for writing types are defined in standards 1–3 above.)	X	X	X	X	X	X
*CCSS.ELA-Literacy.W.3.5 With guidance and support from peers and adults, develop and strengthen writing as needed by planning, revising, and editing. (Editing for conventions should demonstrate command of Language standards 1–3 up to and including grade 3 here.)	X	X	X	X	X	X
*CCSS.ELA-Literacy.W.3.6 With guidance and support from adults, use technology to produce and publish writing (using keyboarding skills) as well as to interact and collaborate with others.	X	X	X	X	X	X

Alignment of New Nonfiction Jacob's Ladder Program to the CCSS-ELA Standards

	A	B	C	D	E	F
Research: Research to Build and Present Knowledge						
CCSS.ELA-Literacy.W.3.7 Conduct short research projects that build knowledge about a topic.				X		
CCSS.ELA-Literacy.W.3.8 Recall information from experiences or gather information from print and digital sources; take brief notes on sources and sort evidence into provided categories.	X			X		
Range of Writing						
CCSS.ELA-Literacy.W.3.10 Write routinely over extended time frames (time for research, reflection, and revision) and shorter time frames (a single sitting or a day or two) for a range of discipline-specific tasks, purposes, and audiences.	X	X	X	X	X	X
Speaking & Listening: Comprehension and Collaboration						
CCSS.ELA-Literacy.SL.3.1 Engage effectively in a range of collaborative discussions (one-on-one, in groups, and teacher-led) with diverse partners on grade 3 topics and texts, building on others' ideas and expressing their own clearly.	X	X	X	X	X	X
CCSS.ELA-Literacy.SL.3.2 Determine the main ideas and supporting details of a text read aloud or information presented in diverse media and formats, including visually, quantitatively, and orally.				X		
CCSS.ELA-Literacy.SL.3.3 Ask and answer questions about information from a speaker, offering appropriate elaboration and detail.	X		X	X		

Appendix C

Alignment of New Nonfiction Jacob's Ladder Program to the CCSS-ELA Standards

	A	B	C	D	E	F
Speaking & Listening: Presentation of Knowledge and Ideas						
CCSS.ELA-Literacy.SL.3.4 Report on a topic or text, tell a story, or recount an experience with appropriate facts and relevant, descriptive details, speaking clearly at an understandable pace.			✗			
CCSS.ELA-Literacy.SL.3.5 Create engaging audio recordings of stories or poems that demonstrate fluid reading at an understandable pace; add visual displays when appropriate to emphasize or enhance certain facts or details.			✗	✗		
CCSS.ELA-Literacy.SL.3.6 Speak in complete sentences when appropriate to task and situation in order to provide requested detail or clarification. (See grade 3 Language standards 1 and 3 here for specific expectations.)	✗	✗	✗	✗	✗	✗
Language						
CCSS.ELA-Literacy.L.3.5 Demonstrate understanding of figurative language, word relationships, and nuances in word meanings.						✗

*These skills are not addressed directly through the program although teachers may wish to extend the writing component of the program to address them.

About the Authors

Tamra Stambaugh, Ph.D., is an assistant research professor in special education and executive director of Programs for Talented Youth at Vanderbilt University. Stambaugh conducts research in gifted education with a focus on students living in rural settings, students of poverty, and curriculum and instructional interventions that promote gifted student learning. She is the coauthor/editor of several books, including *Comprehensive Curriculum for Gifted Learners* (2007; with Joyce VanTassel-Baska); *Overlooked Gems: A National Perspective on Low-Income Promising Students* (2007; with Joyce VanTassel-Baska), *Leading Change in Gifted Education* (2009; with Bronwyn MacFarlane), the Jacob's Ladder Reading Comprehension Program Series (2008, 2009, 2010, 2011, 2012, 2016; with Joyce VanTassel-Baska), *Effective Curriculum for Underserved Gifted Students* (2012; with Kim Chandler), *Serving Gifted Students in Rural Settings* (Legacy Award Winner; with Susannah Wood), and the ELA Lessons for Gifted and Advanced Learners in Grades 6–8 series (2016; with Emily Mofield). Stambaugh has also written numerous articles and book chapters. She frequently provides keynotes, professional development workshops, and consultation to school districts nationally and internationally and shares her work at refereed research conferences. She serves on the National Association for Gifted Children (NAGC) awards and professional standards committees and is a reviewer for leading research journals in the field of gifted education.

Stambaugh is the recipient of several awards including: the Margaret The Lady Thatcher Medallion for scholarship, service, and character from the College of William and Mary School of Education; the Doctoral Student Award, Early Leader Award, and several curriculum awards from the National Association for Gifted Children; the Jo Patterson Service Award and Curriculum Award from the Tennessee Association for Gifted Children; and the Higher Education Award from the Ohio Association for Gifted Children. Stambaugh has received or directed research and service grants totaling more than $7.5 million. Prior to her appointment at Vanderbilt, she was director of grants and special projects at the College of William and Mary, Center for Gifted Education where she earned her Ph.D.

Joyce VanTassel-Baska, Ed.D., is the Jody and Layton Smith Professor Emerita of Education and founding director of the Center for Gifted Education at The College of William and Mary in Virginia where she developed a graduate program and a research and development center in gifted education. She also initiated and directed the Center for Talent Development at Northwestern University. Prior to her work in higher education, Dr. VanTassel-Baska served as the state director of gifted programs for Illinois, as a regional director of a gifted service center in the Chicago area, as coordinator of gifted programs for the Toledo, Ohio public school system, and as a teacher of gifted high school students in English and Latin. She has worked as a consultant on gifted education in all 50 states and for key national groups, including the U.S. Department of Education, National Association of Secondary School Principals, and American Association of School Administrators. She has consulted internationally in Australia, New Zealand, Hungary, Jordan, Singapore, Korea, Hong Kong, China, England, Germany, The Netherlands, Spain, Kazakhstan, Oman, and the United Arab Emirates. She is past president of The Association for the Gifted, the Council for Exceptional Children, the Northwestern University Chapter of Phi Delta Kappa, and the National Association for Gifted Children (NAGC). During her tenure as NAGC president, she oversaw the adoption of the new teacher standards for gifted education, and organized and chaired the National Leadership Conference on Promising and Low-Income Learners.

Dr. VanTassel-Baska has published widely, including 30 books and more than 550 refereed journal articles, book chapters, and scholarly reports. Recent books include: *Content-Based Curriculum for Gifted Learners* (3rd edition; 2016; with Catherine Little), *Patterns and Profiles of Low Income Learners* (2010), *Social and Emotional Curriculum for Gifted and Talented Students* (2009; with Tracy Cross and Rick Olenchak), *Alternative Assessment With Gifted Students* (2008), *Serving Gifted Learners Beyond the Traditional Classroom* (2007), and *Comprehensive Curriculum for Gifted Education* (3rd edition; 2006; with Tamra Stambaugh). Recent curriculum work includes The Jacob's Ladder Reading Comprehension Program (with Tamra Stambaugh), units of study on leadership (with Linda Avery) and on Rome, focusing on its language, history, and art and architecture (with Ariel Baska). She also served as the editor of *Gifted and Talented International*, a research journal of the World Council on Gifted and Talented, for 7 years from 1998–2005.

Dr. VanTassel-Baska has received numerous awards for her work, including the National Association for Gifted Children's Early Leader Award in 1986; the State Council of Higher Education in Virginia Outstanding Faculty Award in 1993; the Phi Beta Kappa faculty award in 1995; the National Association for Gifted Children Distinguished Scholar Award in 1997; the President's Award, World Council on Gifted and Talented Education in 2005; the Distinguished Service Award, CEC-TAG, in 2007; and was inducted as an American Educational Research Association (AERA) Fellow in 2010 along with receiving the Distinguished Service Award from NAGC in the same year. In 2011, she received the Mensa Award for Lifetime Achievement in research and service to gifted education. In 2013, she received the Distinguished Service Award from The World Council on the Gifted and Talented. In 2014, she received the Legacy Award from NAGC for her lifetime contribution to gifted education and a recognition award from Rutgers University for her work in establishing gifted education coursework at that institution. She also has received awards from five states—Ohio, Virginia, Colorado, South Carolina, and Illinois—for her contribution to the field of gifted education in those states. She was selected as a Fulbright Scholar to New Zealand in 2000 and a visiting scholar to Cambridge University in England in 1993. Her major research interests are on the talent development process and effective curricular interventions with the gifted. She has served as principal investigator on 65 grants and contracts totaling more than $15 million, including eight from the United States Department of Education (USDOE). She holds B.A., M.A., M.Ed., and Ed.D. degrees from the University of Toledo, an institution that awarded her its Distinguished Achievement Alumna Award in 2002.

For Product Safety Concerns and Information please contact our EU representative GPSR@taylorandfrancis.com
Taylor & Francis Verlag GmbH, Kaufingerstraße 24, 80331 München, Germany

www.ingramcontent.com/pod-product-compliance
Lightning Source LLC
Chambersburg PA
CBHW081155290426
44108CB00018B/2553